How Airbrushes Work

Steven Leahy

D1567436

Published by:

ArtKulture ~An Imprint of Wolfgang Publications~

PO Box 223 • Stillwater, MN 55082
www.wolfpub.com

BELLEVUE PUBLIC LIBRARY
BELLEVUE, OHIO

Legals

First published in 2009 by Wolfgang Publications Inc.,
PO Box 223, Stillwater MN 55082

© Steven Leahy, 2009

All rights reserved. With the exception of quoting brief passages for the purposes of review no part of this publication may be reproduced without prior written permission from the publisher.

The information in this book is true and complete to the best of our knowledge. All recommendations are made without any guarantee on the part of the author or publisher, who also disclaim any liability incurred in connection with the use of this data or specific details.

We recognize that some words, model names and designations, for example, mentioned herein are the property of the trademark holder. We use them for identification purposes only. This is not an official publication.

ISBN-13: 978-1-929133-71-0
ISBN-10: 1-929133-71-5
Printed and bound in China.

How Airbrushes Work

Acknowledgements

First and foremost, I want to thank my children, Colin, Emily and Matthew for enduring my hibernation during the writing of this book. Their support and understanding were immeasurable and I dedicate this book to them.

Thanks to my parents for being the driving motivational force in seeing that my dream is realized.

Steve Angers at BearAir, without your constant supply of airbrushes and information, this book would have taken far, far longer to complete.

Geoff Carter, how you took the words, photos, charts and illustrations that I threw at you and made sense of them all still boggles my mind. Thank you.

Tim Remus and Wolfgang Publications, thanks to you for taking this seed of an idea and making it a reality.

To all my friends at Airbrush.com and LearnAirbrush.com, for the countless interactions I have enjoyed. They have helped me to grow beyond what I could imagine as an artist.

Finally, to all my former "Introduction to Airbrush" students, the information contained in this book got its start in my mind as I taught that class. Working with so many new artists has given me a far greater understanding of my own art.

Thank you.

Introduction

The use of an airbrush in any kind of work can be transforming. The control that this tool offers, the way that it allows users to express their visions is unique. From imperceptibly smooth fades to machine-like hard edges—the airbrush does it all.

As with so many other tools, getting the most out of this amazing device takes a bit of knowledge and practice. The time spent on the basics, however, will yield fantastic results.

My own journey with the airbrush started in 1988 as a result of a struggle I was having with my college artwork. Each week we would be given a new assignment; each week I would look at the work that I was producing and feel that it just looked unfinished. The colors were thin, faded and uninspiring. Something was not right.

During that time I began looking around for artwork that did inspire me. Something that would help me bridge the gap between where my work was and where I wanted it to be. My attention was constantly being captured by the images of Hajime Sorayama, Michael Cacy and other artists. They all had one thing in common. They all incorporated the airbrush into their work. That was when I decided to get an airbrush and start learning. That was my sophomore year, and by the time I graduated I had gotten a painting accepted into the Society of Illustrators Annual Show in New York.

The airbrush wasn't the reason that my painting got into that show. It was more what the airbrush unlocked in my work that made that show possible for me.

The airbrush gave me the control I was looking for and made me change the paint I used. It gave me more avenues to reach the vision I had for my work.

The purpose of this book is to share the knowledge you need to use the airbrush to reach your vision. Information and examples found on the following pages are designed to get your journey started on the right path, and will allow you to get the most out of the airbrush, regardless of what form of art you are producing. So let the adventure begin!

Chapter One

History of the Airbrush

Airbrush Chronicles

The history of air-propelled paint dates back as far as 16,000 years to the cave paintings in Lascaux, France. Ancient man would take ground pigments and put them in a hollowed out bone or reed. Then, by placing their hands on the cave wall they could blow that pigment out using lung power. The result was a quick, yet extremely accurate image of the artist's hand. It was a perfectly accurate record of the artist. The notion of propelling paint with air survives as a very useful method of delivering paint.

Later artists used what is called a mouth atom-

Closeup of the paint reservoir from Liberty Walkup's air brush. – Nub Graphix

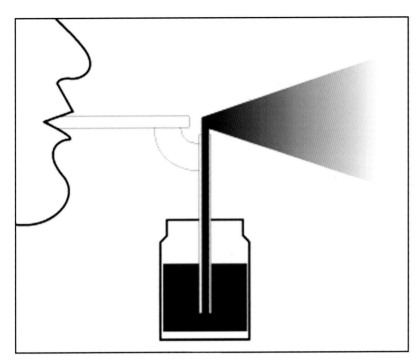

The simple mouth atomizer demonstrates the principles that continue to be used in the airbrushes of today.

izer. Being the first tool to draw paint into the flow of air, the mouth atomizer was the forerunner of the modern airbrush. It was a simple device made up of two tubes connected at a 90-degree angle. The lower tube was placed in a jar that held the liquid paint. The artist would then blow into the other tube. As the air rushed through the upper tube it would create a vacuum at the top of the lower tube that was placed in the paint. This vacuum would draw the paint up to the top where it was sheared off into tiny drops and propelled onto the surface of the object being painted.

There was no better way to spray pigment at the time, and it yielded poor results. The spray pattern was often uncontrolled and inconsistent. Despite its shortcomings, the mouth atomizer is still available today.

In 1882 an inventor named Abner Peeler took the first major step toward pulling all the ideas for propelling paint together, and created the first hand-held tool. Peeler was an avid inventor with more than 100 inventions to his credit, including the typewriter.

Peeler's new invention was named the Paint Distributer, and was created from simple found objects. Two blocks of wood were joined at a right angle, and two small brass plumbing pipes were attached. One fed air to a handmade turbine and the other fed air for the atomization of paint. The paint itself was held in a small jam spoon. The key to Peeler's design was the inclusion of a small sewing needle. The paint from the reservoir was drawn onto this needle and guided into the flow of air so it would be atomized into a fine spray.

Peeler's design came at the perfect time as photography had become extremely popular in the late 1800s. There was a need during that time for a more efficient way to correct and enhance the photographs being taken.

The first public display of the Paint Distributer was at a photography convention in Indianapolis where it was used to retouch a photograph of the inventor himself.

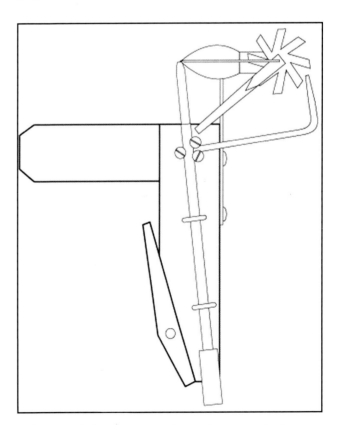

Abner Peeler's 1879 Paint Distributer made the early airbrush a practical device.

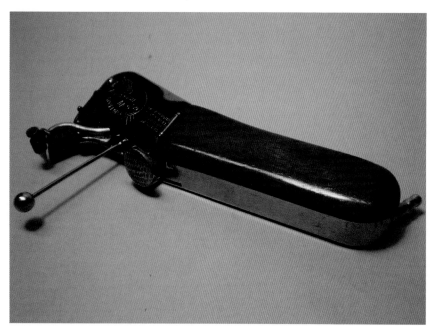

In 1881, Liberty Walkup bought the rights to Peeler's Distributer, made some refinements, and went into full production. — Nub Graphix

Photo retouching at the time was all done by hand, using traditional painting methods. The overall problem was that it was difficult to recreate the texture and the grainy pattern of the photograph by hand. Peeler's invention however, recreated that grainy pattern very well.

This original airbrush received its air from a storage tank near the operator. The artist would fill the tank with compressed air via a set of small foot pumps located directly under the workstation.

Peeler was a prolific inventor, but he was not as skilled as a businessman. In 1882, Peeler found the need to sell his patent for the Distributer. A man named Liberty Walkup saw the potential for the Distributer and bought the patent. Walkup's wife at the time was a professional photo retoucher and was able to give her husband educated feedback on the tool.

The airbrush then went through a period of refinement that included the addition of a walking arm to oscillate the needle, giving his new airbrush even finer control than the older design. In 1883, with the help of investors, Walkup began the Airbrush Manufacturing Company in Chicago, Illinois. This company was dedicated to the new tool. Here the design was further refined to make it easier to mass-produce. The company also offered training in the use of the new tool. This combination of manufacture and education in the same building helped to make the airbrush very popular.

The new airbrush had all its components located inside the body of the tool, yet it was still an external-mix airbrush. This meant that the paint and airflow were mixed outside the airbrush.

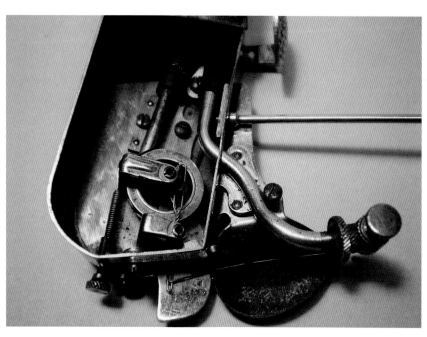

Internal workings of Walkup's design. — Nub Graphix

ENTER CHARLES BURDICK

Burdick was a watercolorist from Chicago who envisioned a different purpose for the airbrush. In 1891 he revolutionized the airbrush by creating a design that internally combined the paint and air. By doing this, Burdick reduced his new airbrush to the size of a fountain pen. This new tool could be held like a pen and operated by the index finger rather than the thumb. This gave the artist a more comfortable and controlled way to work.

The key to the new airbrush's performance was that the simplicity of the paint feed in an internal-mix airbrush made the tool function more reliably. Also, having the needle centered directly in the flow of the paint allows a much greater degree of control over the atomization of the paint.

In 1893 Burdick moved to England and founded the Fountain Brush Company to manufacture his new airbrush, along with highly refined components for clocks and other items. The airbrush began to take on a life of its own, becoming more and more popular. Eventually the company Aerograph was founded to become the sole producer of the airbrush. You can still find the "A" model from Aerograph today.

Peeler's and Walkup's designs can also be found in modern airbrushes. The Paasche AB turbo uses some of the same ideas from the original Walkup designs.

The 1900s saw an explosion in the popularity of the airbrush. Photo retouching had become even more popular and the airbrush was the perfect tool for the job. New companies in America - such as Paasche Airbrush Company, Thayer and Chandler, and Badger Airbrush Companies began dedicated production and refinement of the tool.

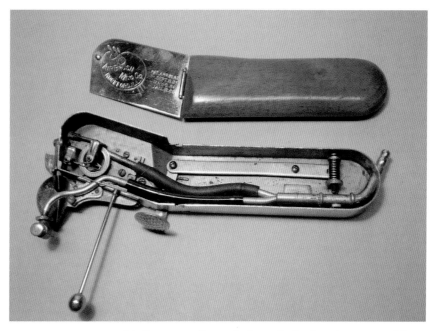

Airflow was directed through the brush using rubber tubing.

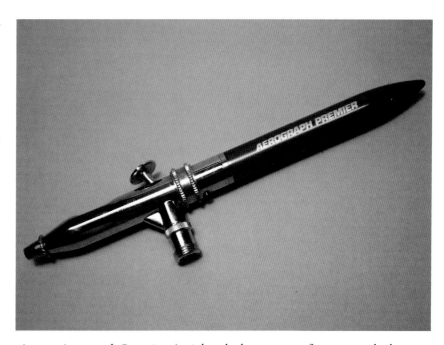

A new Aerograph Premier A airbrush shares many features with the very first Premier A model.

Chapter Two

Basic Function of the Airbrush

Parts That Make Up the Modern Airbrush

Peeler, Walkup and Burdick's original airbrush designs were the foundation and building blocks for all modern airbrushes. Their ideas for delivering paint into a fine stream of air were nearly identical to how airbrushes work today. However, changes have come in the quality and refinement of those components, as well as variations in how some of those parts operate.

An airbrush has two main controls. One determines how much air passes through the brush, a small valve, usually located near the bottom of the airbrush does this. The operator opens the air

Preset handle from a Richpen 213C.

valve, allowing the air to pass through, by depressing the main lever.

The other main component of airbrush operation to be controlled is the paint flow. This control is located in different places on different airbrushes, but the function is the same. It allows paint to be fed at a restricted rate into the stream of air. Once the paint enters the air stream, it travels to the tip of the needle - where it is atomized into a very fine spray.

Understanding the basic functions of these parts can help you accurately determine which extras will give the greatest advantage to your airbrushing. In this chapter we will look at the individual parts of the common airbrush and how the variations in those parts affect the airbrush's performance.

IDENTIFYING THE PARTS

The airbrush handle has a number of purposes. First, it acts as a counterbalance for the rest of the airbrush. When the cup or bottle is filled with paint the brush becomes very front-heavy. Having extra weight in the back can keep things balanced and comfortable. Another function of the handle is to protect the internal parts of the airbrush from damage.

Handles come in several different styles, presenting the prospective buyer with many choices. One option is the preset adjustment. This small dial on the back of the handle restricts the

Standard handle from a Paasche VL.

Cut-away handle from an Iwata Eclipse BCS.

Needles from Iwata HPB (left) and Paasche VL #3 - the finer needle works better with thinner paint.

Needle chuck from Badger 360.

Top: Needle support from an Iwata HPC
Bottom: Needle chuck from Paasche VL

needle's rearward travel. This control is used for repetitive patterns that require the user to release a specific amount of paint each time the trigger is pulled back.

Another option in handles is the cut-away. The cut-away handle has holes, or ports, in the sides. These holes allow the user to pull the needle assembly fully backward without having to remove the needle. This allows blockages of dried paint that are stuck in the airbrush to be cleared quickly.

Needle - This is one of the most important parts of the airbrush. The paint is atomized as it is blown past the tip of a long, very thin and sharp needle. The needle is often characterized by a specific measurement, but this designation is more an indicator of the size of the corresponding nozzle.

The taper of the needle determines how it functions. A long thin taper provides excellent atomization and fine control, yet tends to accumulate dried paint more frequently. A needle with a shorter taper gives excellent paint flow, but with less refinement in the spray quality. This is generally considered better for spraying thicker paint.

Needle chuck - The small nut that holds the needle securely in place is called the needle chuck. This knurled nut is located in the back of the airbrush and is designed to be hand tightened. Overtightening this nut can cause the needle to bind inside the brush and fail to function. To correct this, simply loosen the nut and retighten it until it is snug.

Needle support - This long thin tube guides the needle through the airbrush and aligns it with the nozzle. It is split at the back end, with threads that receive the needle chuck as previously described. During operation of the airbrush, the needle support will move back and forth with the main lever and the needle.

Needle spring - The needle spring provides the tension required to move the needle forward into the closed position when the main lever is released. Different sized springs in different brushes will change the feeling of resistance.

Needle spring adjustment - This threaded piece slips over the needle spring and onto the needle support, and is then threaded directly into the airbrush body. Once in place, the needle spring adjustment compresses the needle spring, which puts the tension on the main lever. When threaded fully in, the needle spring adjustment provides extra resistance on the main lever; loosened it releases that tension, making it easier to pull the main lever back. Ultimately, the user's personal preference determines where this adjustment is set.

Auxiliary lever - In a double-action airbrush the auxiliary lever is a small curved piece that transfers the movement of the main lever to the needle support. Without this piece there would be very little control of the flow of paint into the airbrush. In some models the auxiliary lever is attached directly to the needle support on a small pivot pin.

Main lever - Also referred to as the trigger, the main lever is the primary control of the airbrush. The bottom of the main lever makes contact in the floor of the airbrush with the air valve. Pressing the main lever down pushes the air valve pin, which in turn opens the air valve. In some models the air valve pin is attached directly to the main lever.

The backside of the main lever also makes contact with the auxiliary lever and, in a double-action airbrush, pulling back introduces the paint flow.

The trigger pad at the top of the main lever is available in a huge number of variations, depending on the model. Generally they are scalloped on the bottom rear of the pad to allow the main lever to be pulled to the farthest back position. This scallop can also be a good way to help you determine which is front and back when reassembling the airbrush.

Some airbrushes, such as the Paasche VL and the DeVilbiss "Dagger" (DAGR), have removable trigger pads that can be exchanged for custom pads.

Although not recommended by any manufacturer, the main lever can be ground, polished and customized as well. While this will allow the user to tailor the feel of the main lever pad, its drawback is that removing the chrome from the pad

Top: Needle spring from Iwata Revolution CR Bottom: Needle spring adjustment from Iwata HPC Plus.

Needle spring adjustment from Richpen 213C.

Auxiliary lever from Badger 360 Universal.

Auxiliary lever attached to the needle support from Iwata Revolution CR.

Main lever from a Richpen 213C.

Main lever with air valve pin attached from Iwata HP-BC.

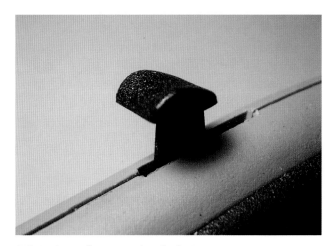

Main lever from an Aztek 470.

Main lever from a Badger 100.

Multiple trigger pads are available for the DeVilbiss DAGR (also known as "dagger").

Custom hand ground and polished Richpen 213C Main Lever.

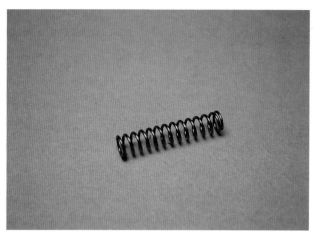

Air valve spring from an Iwata Custom Micron SB.

Teflon needle seal from a Richpen 213C.

The air valve nut from an Iwata Custom Micron SB.

Air valve pin and O-ring.

The air valve is adjusted (in) for maximum resistance in this Iwata Custom Micron SB.

The same Iwata Custom Micron SB now has the air valve adjusted (out) for minimum resistance.

Standard needle cap from Iwata Revolution CR..

Crown needle cap for an Iwata Custom Micron C.

exposes the less durable brass underneath. Because it is relatively inexpensive and easy to replace, the trigger pad is a popular part to customize.

Needle seal - This small seal is located inside the airbrush, usually just behind the paint reservoir. The needle seal's job is to stop paint from flowing backwards into the body of the airbrush. It is usually held in place by a threaded nut that can be adjusted to compress the needle seal for a perfect fit. Needle seals can be made of a solvent-resistant rubber or solvent-proof Teflon. The latter is more suited for work with enamels and solvent-based automotive paints.

Air valve - The air valve itself is a long thin pin that has a rubber O-ring mounted in its center. This pin both guides the seal and provides the contact for the air valve pin above. The air valve O-ring, while solvent resistant, is rarely solvent-proof. Care must be taken never to submerge the airbrush in solvents when cleaning. Over time this will cause deterioration of the O-ring.

Air valve spring - The air valve spring performs the same function for the air valve that the needle spring does for the needle. This small spring provides backpressure that returns the air valve to the closed position (up) when the main lever is released.

Air valve nut - The air valve nut threads into the bottom of the air valve housing and holds all the air valve components together. This small nut is also adjustable. The farther it is threaded into the air valve housing, the greater the resistance on the air valve. Some users prefer more resistance when pressing the main lever down; some prefer less. It is all about the comfort of the user during operation.

Needle cap – The purpose of the needle cap is to protect the tip of the needle that extends out from the front of the airbrush. The types and styles of needle caps are endless. The standard cone-shaped caps provide the most protection for the needle, but they compromise the airbrush's detail performance. Ported and crown needle caps offer less protection, yet disperse air better giving better up close performance. Some needle caps allow adjustment of the airflow across the tip of the airbrush. The needle cap however, is not required for the operation of the airbrush. It can be removed completely, resulting in superior, tight detail control, but this leaves the tip of the needle fully exposed to the risk of accidental damage.

Most manufacturers probably will take the safe route and tell you to keep the cap on, but few artists actually use it in place at all times, if ever. When the inevitable accident occurs, you will need the repair instructions we present later in this book.

Nozzle cap - The nozzle cap directs the air that moves through the airbrush down across the tip of the nozzle. Its opening is precisely machined just larger than the diameter of the nozzle. Care should be taken when handling this small piece. Any damage to the opening will compromise the performance of the airbrush. In addition, any break in the seal between the nozzle cap and the body of the airbrush will compromise the airbrush's ability to function by also breaking the vacuum within the cap.

Air cap - The air cap directs the airflow from the body of the airbrush into the nozzle cap. Some airbrushes offer multiple sizes of nozzle caps and nozzles, yet the air cap is generally universal for each of the different sizes.

Nozzle - Also known as the tip, the nozzle is truly the heart of the airbrush. This very small cone shaped piece directs the paint onto the needle. Nozzles are identified in several ways. The size of the opening at the tip of the nozzle determines the viscosity of material that it is designed to handle, and the refinement of the spray pattern.

European and Japanese manufacturers will list the exact size of the nozzle, usually in millimeters. The smallest of openings are in the .1mm to .2mm range. These incredibly small nozzles are designed to process very thin material such as inks, dyes and automotive candies. While offering amazingly fine atomization, they also tend to clog more often if the viscosity of the paint is too thick.

The .3mm to .4mm range offers very fine control due to the slightly larger opening, and is more forgiving of the thickness of the paint. This size is

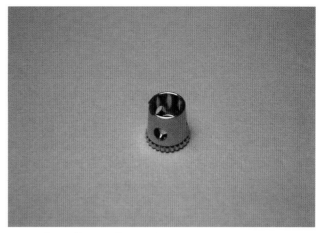
Ported needle cap for Richpen 213C.

Airflow across the tip of the nozzle can be controlled using one of these spray regulators on a Badger 100.

Nozzle cap from Richpen 213C.

Air cap from DeVilbiss DAGR.

perfectly suited for materials such as acrylic paints, automotive basecoats and makeup.

The .5mm to .7mm range is designed to process thicker media such as fabric paint. Even though these nozzles are larger in size, they still offer a great amount of control, especially with higher air pressures. Finally, the .8mm to 1mm sizes are designed for the thickest paints, such as metallics and pearls, as well as latex-based paint.

Most American made nozzles use a numbering system to designate their sizes. In some instances the nozzle size will be indicated by #1 for fine, #3 for medium and #5 for a large nozzle opening. It is also common in American airbrushes to find the designations of "Fine," "Medium" and "Heavy." You can find out the actual measurements by checking with the individual manufacturers. Knowing these measurements will help you match the nozzle size to your job.

The second important aspect regarding the nozzle is how it seats in the body of the airbrush. Most nozzles are secured in one of two ways.

The first is referred to as a self-centering or self-seating nozzle. This type of nozzle simply sits in the body of the airbrush and is held in place by the air cap. Because the threads of the air cap are heavy duty, this style of airbrush operates very well at higher pressures.

Self-centering nozzle from Iwata HP-BCS.

The other type of nozzle has the threads machined onto the nozzle itself. The nozzle then threads directly into the body of the airbrush for a very secure fit. The advantage of this design is that with such a precise fit the nozzle can be manufactured extremely small for finer atomization of paint - and the greatest amount of control. The main disadvantage to this style is its high cost of production. Extra care must also be taken when installing this style to prevent damage to the components.

Body - The body of the airbrush is the foundation for all the other parts. Generally, airbrushes are nickel and chrome plated brass, although some airbrushes, such as the Aztek, have bodies made of composite materials.

Extra care should always be taken when handling the body of the airbrush. Damaged threads on the body usually are not repairable, and it is just as expensive to replace most manufacturers' bodies as it is to purchase an entire airbrush.

Color cup - Gravity-fed airbrushes have a paint reservoir mounted directly to the top of the airbrush. These cups often include an unthreaded cap to keep the paint inside the cup. Each of these caps has a small vent hole in it that allows air to enter the cup as the paint is depleted. If the hole were not there, as the paint was drawn out of the cup it would create a vacuum and eventually stop the flow of paint.

Becoming familiar with the basic parts of the airbrush will help you tremendously in the operation of the tool, as well as enabling you to diagnose and correct problems that arise. Knowing the names and functions of these parts will also make your life so much easier when you need to order new parts. Keep in mind that variations in the style of these parts, and the names used by different manufacturers will require a little cross referencing, but knowing the function of each part will make that translation much easier.

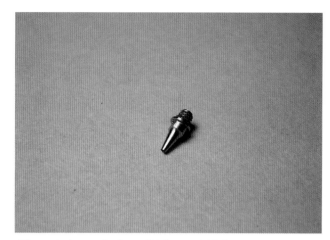

Threaded nozzle from Richpen 112A.

Color cup from Badger 100.

Color cup cap from Iwata HPC.

Chapter Three

Paint Feed Types

Different Ways That Paint Is Fed

The method in which paint feeds onto the needle determines a large part of the airbrush's performance. One method is not universally better than another. Rather, the job it is required to do will determine which feed type is best suited for the task. As you begin to purchase and use airbrushes, you probably will find the need for both the gravity-fed and siphon-fed styles of brushes. This chapter will look at the characteristics, advantages and disadvantages of each kind of paint feed.

THE GRAVITY-FEED AIRBRUSH

In a gravity-feed airbrush, the paint reservoir is mounted directly on the top of the airbrush

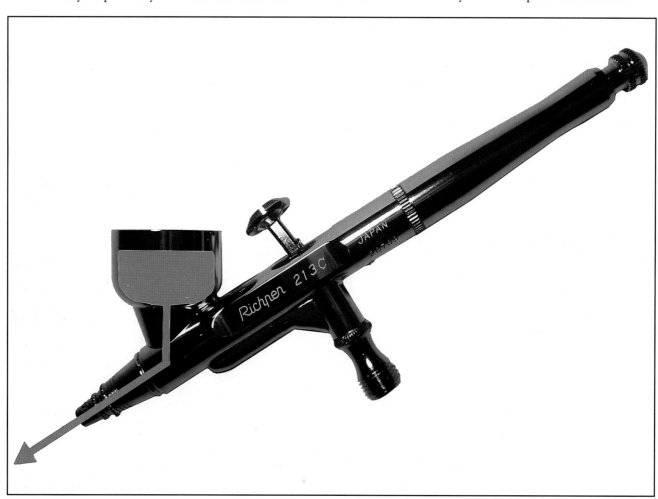

Diagram of the paint flow in a gravity-feed airbrush.

body, between the air cap and the main lever. In some instances, this reservoir is as simple as a slot in the top of the body. Regardless of the size or shape of the reservoir or color cup, the bottom of this cup actually includes a portion of the body of the airbrush. As the needle passes through this section of the airbrush body it picks up paint and transfers it to the tip of the needle for atomization. While the vacuum that is created in the front of the airbrush draws the paint down the needle, the gravity of the paint helps the feed as well. The addition of gravity to the siphoning action of the vacuum in the front of the airbrush enables this type of airbrush to operate at a lower air pressure.

Take a look inside the color cup of an Iwata HPC Plus.

Lower pressure, combined with thinner paint, can give the artist incredible control. As a result, airbrush manufacturers have tailored the gravity-feed airbrush for just this purpose. Most gravity-feed airbrushes offer much smaller nozzles and needles. Their matching nozzle caps are designed to focus the air precisely across these micro nozzles.

As noted earlier, the color cups come in a number of different shapes and sizes. A small open slot in the top of the airbrush, while only holding 1/16th of an ounce of paint, creates no visual obstruction for the user who needs to be directly on top of the surface being painted. This is a great advantage over other airbrushes when

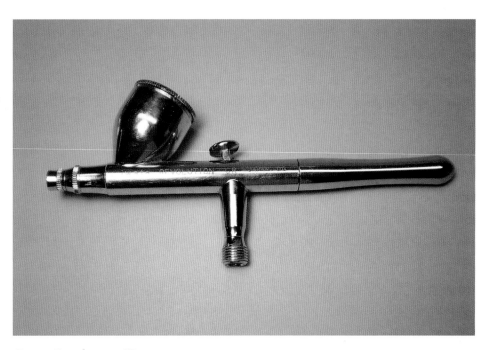

Iwata Revolution CR.

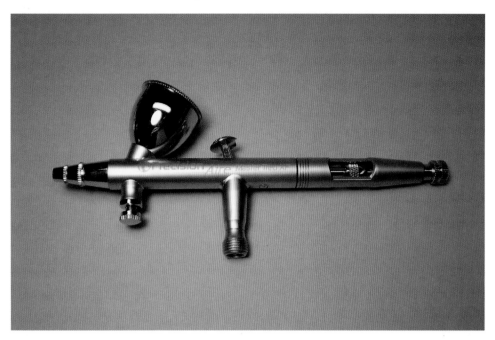

PrecisionAire Master Treo.

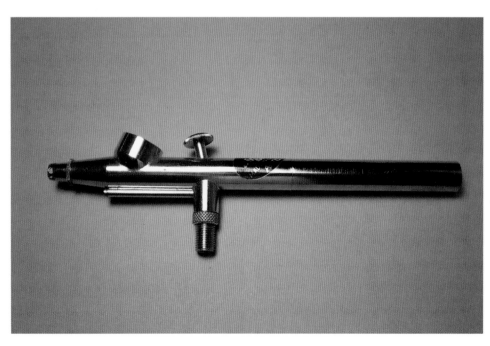

Efbe Artis 1.

painting fingernails, for example.

Some gravity-feed air-brushes, such as the DeVilbiss DAGR, have removable color cups that can be swapped out according to the needs of the job.

SIPHON-FEED AIRBRUSH

The siphon feed air-brush has a larger bottle than the others and hangs below the airbrush. This bottle's paint-feed tube extends down to the bottom of the bottle. As the air is introduced, a vacuum is created that draws paint up from the bottle onto the needle. It is then carried forward, where it is atomized and sprayed out of the airbrush. This type of paint-feed applies the same physics that the simple mouth atomizer uses. Because it relies on air pressure to do the work, it takes a larger amount of pressure to operate the airbrush.

Again, manufacturers saw this and tailored most siphon airbrushes for operation with thicker paints, in greater vouges. T-shirt painting is a classic example of a use for which a brush like this is tailor made.

One of the advantages to the siphon feed air-brush is that it can hold far more material than a gravity feed brush. It also can be run at considerably higher pressures than other airbrushes, making it an excellent candidate for processing thicker paints. Finally, because their components are not as technically challenging to manufacture, they tend to be less expensive to purchase and maintain.

Their disadvantage is that the bottle that hangs below the airbrush can interfere with the work surface, if that surface is not mounted vertically.

SIDE-FEED AIRBRUSH

Finally, this hybrid type falls between the other two. The side-feed airbrush draws its material from a cup, or bottle, mounted on the side of the brush. While this type of feed is technically considered to be a siphon-feed, it has enough unique features to allow it to stand alone. The first characteristic is that the fluid reservoirs mounted on the side of the airbrush are removable. That allows a nearly limitless number of options in the style of reservoir that can be used. Cups with the fluid feed on the bottom will perform in a manner similar to a gravity-feed airbrush; a larger bottle will work more like a siphon-feed airbrush.

Another advantage to the side-feed is that the cup can be rotated front to back allowing the airbrush to be operated horizontally, vertically or even straight up. Vision of the work surface is also not as obstructed as it sometime is with a gravity-feed airbrush. Mounting the cup on the

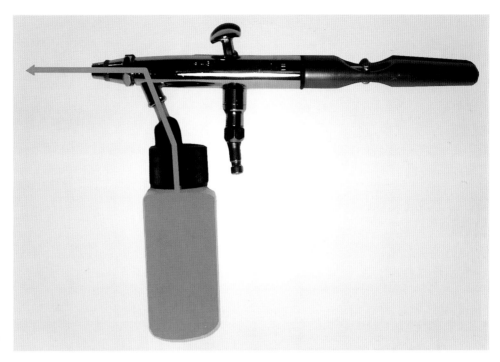

Diagram of the paint flow in a siphon-feed airbrush.

Siphon-feed bottle assembly.

Chapter Four

Main Lever Types

How Primary Controls Vary

The main lever, sometimes called the trigger, is the primary means of control for an airbrush. Depending on the type of airbrush, you can use it to do everything from adjusting the amount of paint being sprayed to allowing the flow of air through the brush. In this chapter we will not only look at the different functions the main lever can perform, but also take a more in-depth look at the different styles available.

The main lever of most airbrushes is still

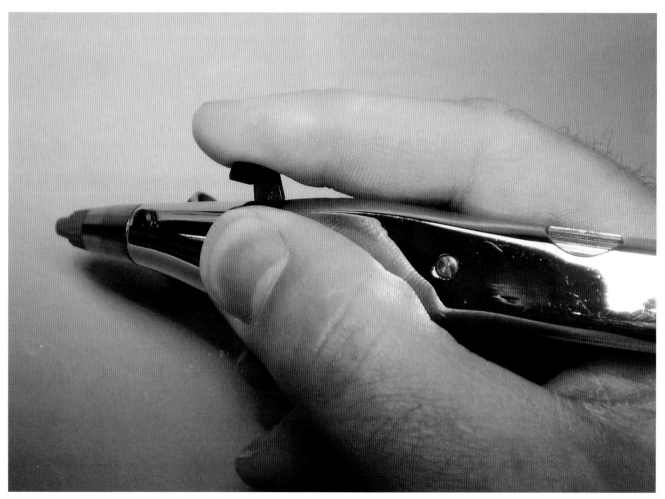

Index finger placement on a standard dual-action trigger - press down for air first, then pull back for paint.

located on the top of the airbrush, similar to Burdick's original design. It is generally operated with the tip of the index finger. Some crossover airbrushes use a trigger below the body of the brush, but these also are intended for index-finger operation. The functions that the main lever controls determine the type of airbrush to which it belongs.

SINGLE-ACTION AIRBRUSH

The first is the single-action airbrush. The main lever of a single-action airbrush only introduces airflow into the brush. When the main lever is pressed down the air valve below it is opened, allowing air to pass through the airbrush.

The flow of paint in a single-action airbrush is controlled by a separate adjustment. In the majority of these, the paint control is located in the back of the airbrush handle. Turning this paint flow adjustment withdraws the needle and allows paint to flow through the airbrush.

Purchasing a single-action airbrush is a very good choice if the jobs you plan will require a consistent rate of paint flow. Repetitive, or large-scale, fluid application is easily accomplished with today's single-action airbrushes.

There is a common misconception that single-action airbrushes are better to learn with. In fact, the opposite is usually the case. Because a single-action airbrush has separate air and paint controls, using this style of airbrush actually requires two hands. While it is initially easier to get paint spraying with a single-action airbrush, learning on one will limit your control later on.

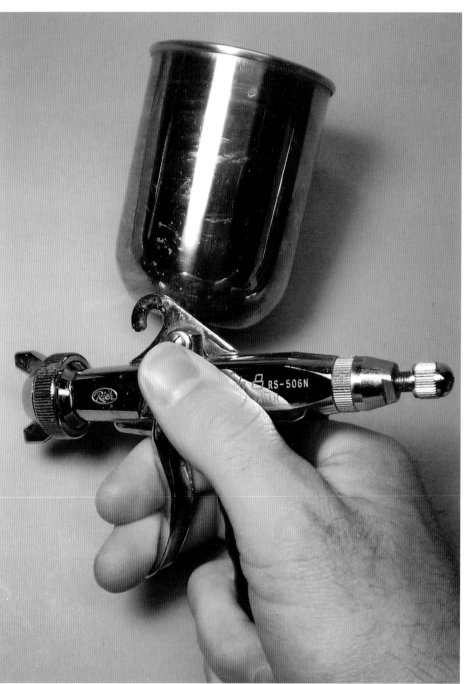

Index finger placement on a fixed-dual-action spray gun is shown. This trigger only pulls back - first 1/4 of travel is air only; beyond that, paint is introduced.

DOUBLE-ACTION AIRBRUSH

The second type of airbrush is called the double-action. In this style, the main lever is pushed down to introduce airflow the same way as one would with the single-action airbrush. The double-action is so named because the trigger can also be pulled backward. By carefully drawing the main lever back - after pressing it down - the operator can slowly introduce fluid into the airflow. The farther the main lever is drawn back, the higher the rate of fluid flow.

Because both controls are operated with one finger, the double-action airbrush is an excellent choice when extreme control is desired. The misconception about the double-action airbrush is that it is difficult to learn. While the amount of air can be controlled by how far the main lever is depressed, in normal operation the main lever is pushed all the way down, allowing the full amount of air to pass. The real control of the airbrush then comes from regulating the amount of paint by moving the lever forward or back. Remembering this simplifies the controls of the double-action airbrush considerably.

FIXED DOUBLE-ACTION AIRBRUSH

The third type of trigger control comes from the larger spray guns. In a fixed double-action airbrush, the air and fluid are still controlled with the main lever, yet they are linked in a different manner from the double-action airbrush. As the main lever is drawn back, the airflow is immediately introduced. As the operator slowly draws the main lever back farther, the paint is introduced. Spray guns operate on the same principle.

Fixed double-action airbrushes are primarily of the trigger type. These airbrushes offer the user a very different manner of control that may be ergonomically perfect for certain applications.

MAIN LEVER PADS

These come in a number of styles. All are designed to provide a non-slip surface for the operator's finger. These pads may be scalloped,

Revell single-action airbrush - the main lever controls air only.

grooved or smooth.

Make sure that the main lever pad is comfortable. An uncomfortable pad can cause fatigue. Check with the manufacturer of your airbrush if you find that the main lever pad is uncomfortable. Some airbrushes have optional main lever pads in different styles that you may find more comfortable. Some manufactures have also created rubber trigger pads for added comfort. Finally, it is possible to modify the main lever pad on your own. Modifications as extensive as grinding and polishing, to something as simple as a small piece of adhesive foam, may make the main lever pad perfect for your needs. Bear in mind that few manufacturers will warrantee an airbrush that is altered in any way.

A variation of the single-action main lever.

The bottom of the main lever also makes contact with the air valve pin in several ways. This contact determines the airbrush's sensitivity as the main lever is depressed to start the airflow. In a double-action airbrush, this contact also determines the smoothness of the

Paint control adjustment is on the handle of this single-action airbrush.

Dual-action airbrush with index finger in the forward position; pressing down allows airflow without paint.

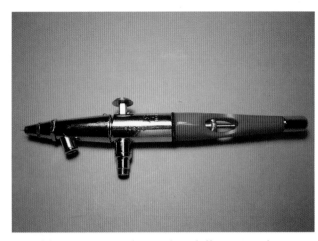

Double-action Paasche VL has different sized interchangeable tips and needles for different viscosities of paint.

When the trigger is in the down, rear position both air and paint are allowed to flow.

Trigger on a fixed double-action in the "air only" position.

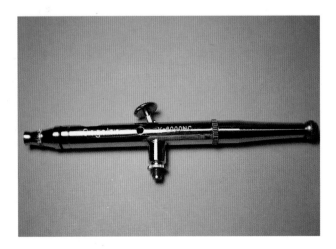

The Sogolee V6000 is an inexpensive imported double-action airbrush.

Trigger on a fixed double-action drawn all the way back for full paint flow.

paint flow. Some air-brushes use a pair of rocker pins that seat in a small cradle in the floor of the brush. In other designs the actual shaft of the main lever pivots on the air valve itself. Finally, some main lever designs have the air valve pin attached to the bottom of the main lever. While each of these styles is very common, being aware of the differences will help you find the ones that feel best to you as you look for and purchase additional airbrushes.

A small assortment of main lever pads shows some of the variety available.

Three of the different types of contacts that connect the main levers to their respective air valves.

Chapter Five

Paint and Air Mixture Types

Advantages and Disadvantages

The paint and air can mix in an airbrush in two ways. In an external-mix airbrush, the paint and air come together at the tip of the airbrush from two separate passageways. In an internal-mix airbrush, the paint and air mix together inside the body of the airbrush. While Burdick is credited with the creation of the first true internal-mix airbrush, both Walkup's and Peeler's designs have more in common with the internal-mix airbrush than an external-mix.

The external-mix airbrush is a true descendant of the mouth atomizer. In the mouth atom-

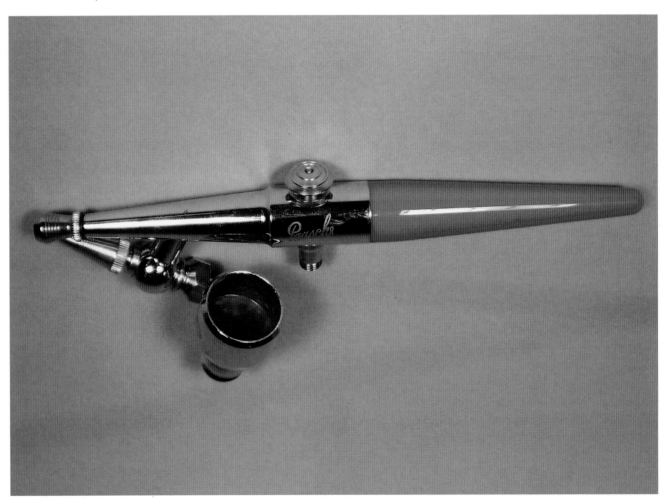

External-mix Paasche H.

izer one tube extended down into the jar of fluid, and the operator blew into the other tube to create the vacuum that drew the fluid up and atomized it.

External-mix airbrushes use exactly the same process. Two tubes come together at a point, one extending into a fluid bottle and the other connected to the air valve. Just as the mouth atomizer produces a coarse and unrefined spray, most external mix airbrushes produce a fairly coarse spray as compared to the internal-mix airbrushes.

Some external-mix airbrushes, however, have become quite refined. Models such as the Paasche H have developed a needle-like cone that delivers the paint in a very controlled way. The overall advantage of the external-mix airbrushes is that they are simple designs, which makes them extremely durable and easy to maintain. Also, because the design of these airbrushes is simple they are inexpensive to manufacture and purchase.

The main drawback however, is that they offer a generally poor quality of spray. They are ideal however, for bulk general spraying. When a fluid needs to be applied with more direction than a spray can do, yet not with as much control as a higher quality airbrush, the external-mix airbrush is usually a great choice. An example of this

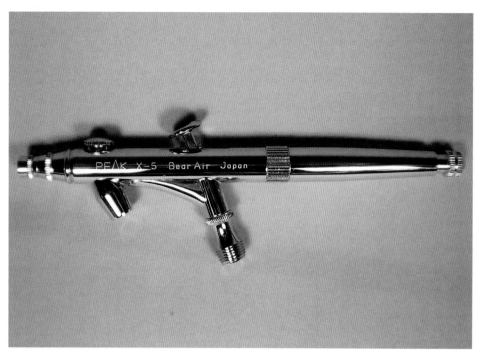

Internal-mix Peak X-5.

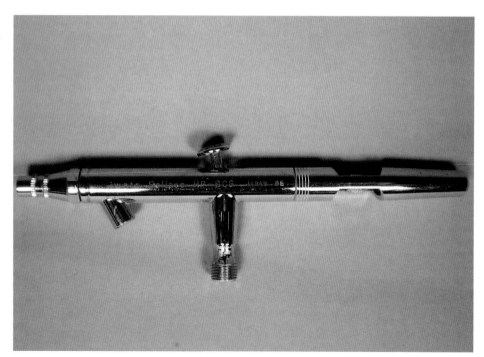

Internal-mix Iwata Eclipse BCS.

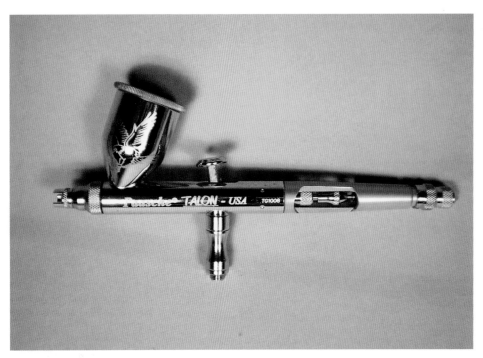

Internal-mix Paasche Talon.

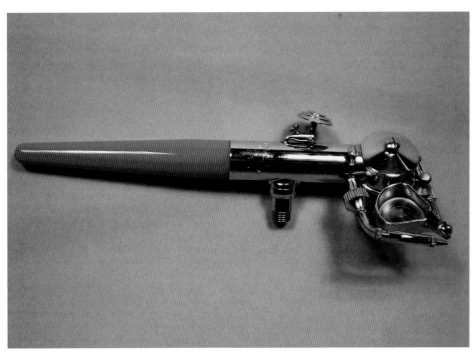

Paasche AB Turbo.

type of application is a ceramist who needs to apply glazes, or someone who repairs furniture and needs to blend colors, or for spray-on tanning applications. These are all examples of applications where the control of an airbrush will work very well, yet the refinement of the spray is not a great concern.

The other more common means of mixing paint and air in today's airbrushes is with the internal-mix design. In this style of airbrush, the paint and air both travel through the body. What makes the internal-mix airbrush work so well is the way the paint and air actually mix.

The air is directed through the airbrush into the air cap. The air cap then funnels the air into the nozzle cap. From there the air is forced out of the nozzle cap where it meets the nozzle and the needle of the airbrush. The paint travels through the airbrush to the end of the nozzle where it continues out onto the tip of the needle. There the perfect cone of air that is created by the nozzle cap atomizes the paint. The nozzle cap opening in some detail airbrushes can be as small as .2mm across. This tiny opening allows the user to tightly focus the air evenly around the needle.

As the internal-mix airbrush is the opposite of the external-mix airbrush, so are the advantages and disadvantages. The design of an internal-mix brush is generally more complex than the internal-mix, making them more expensive to purchase on average. In addition, problems with an internal-mix airbrush can be more subtle, and troubleshooting somewhat trickier.

The obvious advantage though, is the incredible refinement of spray quality that results from using this kind of airbrush. Pinpoint accuracy of spray can be achieved consistently.

The first airbrush from Walkup, Peeler's Paint Distributer, and the modern Paasche AB Turbo have many characteristics in common with an internal-mix airbrush, even though each of these technically mixes the paint and air outside of the body. These airbrushes operate without the fluid tip, or nozzle found in standard internal-mix airbrushes, which allows them to stand in a category all of their own.

The key, as always, when deciding which style of airbrush to buy is to understand the job you expect it to do. Let's say you are refinishing ceramic bathtubs, and you find that an airbrush would be the perfect complement to the heavier duty spray equipment you are using. Following the tried and true rule of, "You get what you pay for," you purchase the Paasche AB Turbo. It is, after all, the most expensive in the case full of airbrushes at the store. You load your pricey purchase with the heavy ceramic glaze that is used for your restoration, and seconds later the airbrush locks up and refuses to operate.

Fortunately, you won't make that mistake because you already know the advantages of the different paint feed, mix and trigger types. And you have found that the single-action, external-mix Paasche H model airbrush, for example, would perform perfectly at a fifth of the cost.

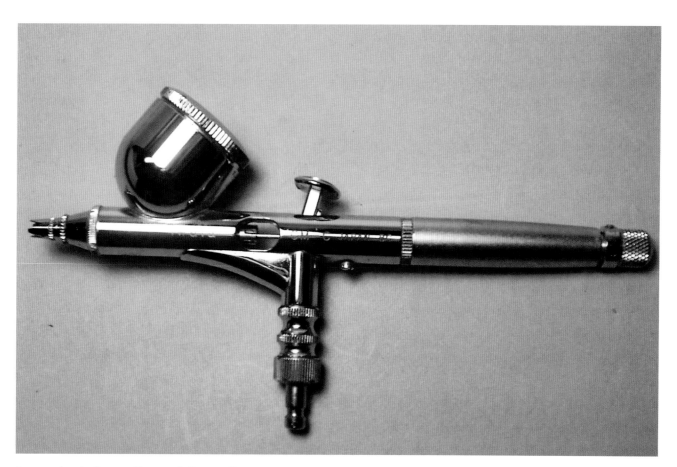

Internal-mix Iwata Custom Micron C.

Paasche #5 VL airbrush.

Remember that these are general guidelines to help you to choose the nozzle size that is best for what you plan to spray. A .3 millimeter nozzle can process thin materials such as ink, yet still handle the thicker viscosity of textile paint. Knowing how the size of the nozzle will react to the materials you use will help you coax your airbrush through many different jobs.

The next important aspect of how the nozzle operates is how it sits in the airbrush itself. The nozzle is held into the airbrush in one of two ways.

Threaded nozzles - In the first style, the nozzle threads directly into the body of the airbrush. This connection is extremely accurate, secure and airtight, making it ideal for airbrushes that are to be used for tight control and high atomization.

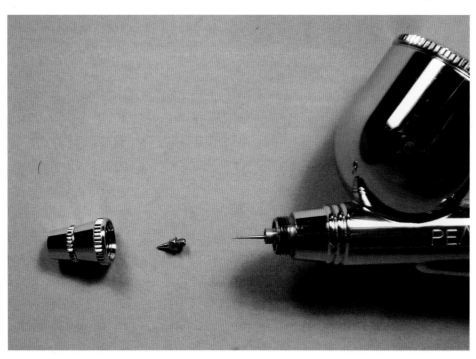

Threaded nozzle removed from the Peak C5.

The disadvantage is that this type of nozzle is not easy to machine. This makes replacement costs about three to four times higher than the cost of the other style of nozzle. In addition, the threaded nozzles are very delicate and can easily be damaged. Their performance, however, far outweighs their drawbacks.

Self-centering nozzle - The second type of nozzle is the self-centering or self-seating nozzle. In this style, the bullet-shaped nozzle fits directly into the body of the airbrush. The threaded air cap is then tightened down

40

Threaded nozzle secured in the Peak C5.

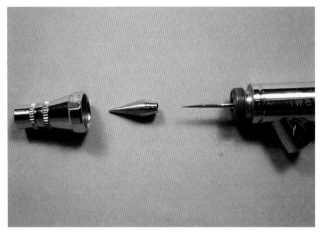

Self-centering nozzle removed from the Iwata Eclipse BCS.

to create an airtight seal. This type of nozzle cannot be machined with an opening of smaller than .5 millimeters. This means production costs and consumer price are lower than the threaded nozzle. By having slightly larger nozzle openings and using the larger threads of the air cap to hold them in place, airbrushes with these types of nozzles are well suited for higher air pressures and thicker paints. Lower maintenance costs also help to make this style of nozzle very popular in workhorse type airbrushes.

Hybrid nozzle - A hybrid style of nozzle, designed to offer the best of both worlds, has recently emerged. This new design mounts a threaded nozzle onto the body of a self-centered nozzle. The result is a nozzle that shares the better features of both styles. Airbrushes such as the DeVilbiss DAGR and the Iwata Eclipse CS both use this new style of nozzle.

Application - When you buy an airbrush designed for a particular application, the style of the included nozzle is usually matched correctly for that use. Nonetheless, understanding the characteristics of the nozzle that comes with an airbrush will help you fine tune both maintenance and performance along the way.

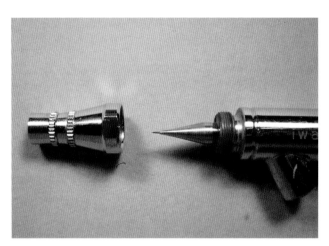

Self centering Iwata Eclipse nozzle in place.

Joint (hybrid) nozzle from the DeVilbiss DAGR.

Chapter Seven

Airbrush Adjustments

Make Your Job Go More Smoothly

The modern airbrush has been defined by its versatility and ease of use. In an ongoing effort to tailor their product to each user's needs, airbrush manufacturers have introduced several different ways to customize each model's capabilities. This chapter will look at the different adjustments that can be found on airbrushes today and how these adjustments affect your work.

Nearly all of the adjustments listed here may be selected according to the personal preferences of the user. Artists will find that different adjustments can be made to better match their individual styles. What may work well for one user may not be comfortable for another. Knowing what

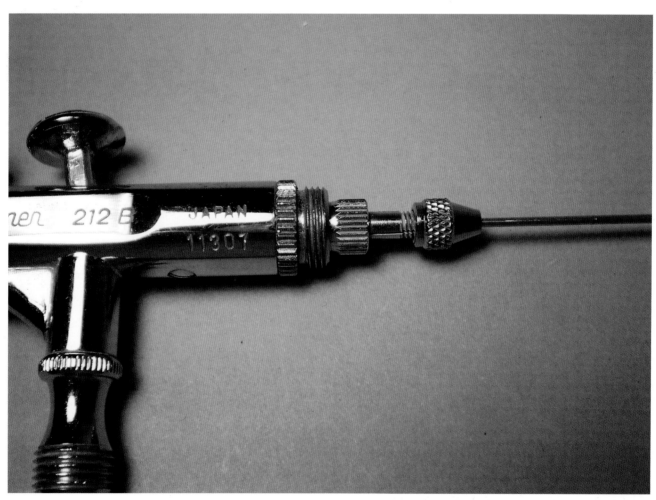

Richpen 212B needle guide at maximum tension.

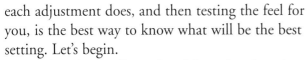

Badger 100 needle spring assembly.

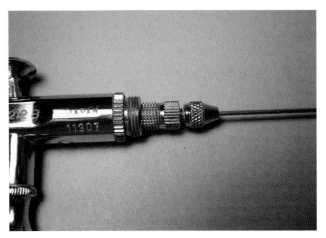

Richpen 212B needle guide at minimum tension.

Iwata HP-CH air valve nut at maximum tension.

Iwata HP-CH air valve nut at minimum tension.

each adjustment does, and then testing the feel for you, is the best way to know what will be the best setting. Let's begin.

Within the needle guide of the airbrush is the needle spring. The amount of compression on this spring determines the resistance to the forward and backward movement of the main lever. Screwing this adjustment into the body of the airbrush compresses the needle spring, putting more resistance on the main lever.

There are two schools of thought regarding the use of this resistance. Higher pressure, or greater resistance, on the main lever can be a good thing when doing tight, small detail painting. This resistance can give you greater control over the spray. However, the other side of the coin is that less resistance can often be better for small, detail

Paasche VL slotted air valve nut.

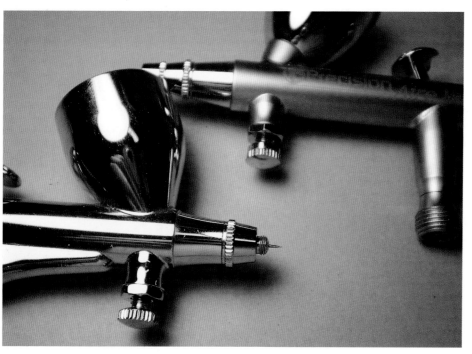

PrecisionAire Master Treo and Iwata HP-CH air control valves.

painting. With less resistance on the trigger, the operator can use a lighter touch. As noted earlier, this adjustment has no standard, correct setting. The best thing to do is set it at the midway point, try it out, and adjust from there.

In certain airbrushes, such as the Badger Model 100, the needle spring is inside a guide assembly. The adjustment is done with a small compression nut at the end of the assembly, but the results are exactly the same.

As the compression of the needle spring affects the resistance on the forward and backward movement of the main lever, so does the air valve spring control the resistance to its up and down motion. In normal operation, given the nature of the air valve itself, it is uncommon to control the flow of air through the air valve with the main lever.

Changing the amount of tension here, however, can improve the comfort of the airbrush's operation. If the operator will be using the airbrush for long periods of time a lighter touch, or less resistance, may be desired to reduce fatigue. This adjustment can be found on the bottom of the airbrush where the air valve screws onto the air hose. Adjust the small air valve nut by inserting the points of a pair of tweezers into the slots on the nut and turning. In some airbrushes, such as the Paasche VL, the air valve nut is adjusted using a small screwdriver. In either style, the more the nut is screwed into the air valve, the greater the tension on the air valve spring and the more resistance on the lever.

In the Iwata HP-CH, the PrecisionAire Master Treo, and other such airbrushes a small adjustable air valve has been installed directly below the color cup. This valve is designed to give the user a measure of control over the flow of air that is difficult to attain simply by depressing the main lever. As the adjustment is turned a small needle valve inside the airbrush gradually restricts the flow of air to the nozzle. This is an advantage when working up close, and with thinner materials. This adjustment also is more convenient than moving the compressor's regulator each time an adjustment is needed.

The Badger 100, and some similar airbrushes, have a spray regulator as part of the front end of the airbrush. This adjustable cap can be loosened to allow more airflow across the nozzle, or tightened to allow less. As with the MAC Valve on the Iwata HP-CH, this adjustment is used to help match the airflow with the specific viscosity of the material that is being sprayed.

Most airbrushes can be operated with their needle caps removed. If the airbrush is used very close to the surface with the needle cap in place, air will bounce off the work surface and back into the needle cap.

Needle cap removed from an Iwata HP-CH.

Nozzle cap removed from an Iwata Micron SB for spatter effect.

The adjustment just forward of the main lever on the Paasche VL presets the main lever in the open position.

This bouncing air will disturb the quality of the spray that is exiting. Removing the needle cap eliminates this problem. With this protective cap removed the air is dispersed from the airbrush much more easily. The needle cap however, also protects the tip of the needle and its removal increases the risk of damaging the tip. By taking care to protect the needle, most users find that the improvement in the spray quality of the airbrush while working with extreme details far outweighs the risk. Some airbrushes are supplied with ported or crown shapes needle caps, but nothing matches the performance of an airbrush with the needle cap removed.

The airbrush has the unique ability to spatter paint as well as to atomize it finely. This spattering of large droplets of paint can create a very textural pattern, yet the airbrush does this with surprising control. To spatter paint with an airbrush, the airflow around the nozzle must be less focused. Removing the airbrush's air cap does this. Because the air cap funnels the airflow directly down to the nozzle, removing it will allow the air to freely exit the front of the airbrush. While this general airflow will blow the paint off the needle, it will not have the focus to atomize it. The result is a very controlled spatter pattern. Increasing the air pressure will make the spatter pattern finer.

Badger 100 single-action adjustment.

Without the air cap in place the airbrush will not create the vacuum that draws the paint out of the cup. Paint must be manually fed onto the needle by rocking the main lever fully back to allow the paint to flow onto the needle, and then forward to allow the air to spatter it. The Aztek series of airbrushes offers a specific nozzle that will only spatter paint, thus making this process very easy.

Some double-action airbrushes, such as the Paasche VL and the Badger Model 100, have the ability to operate as either double-action or single-action airbrushes. This is done in both instances by a small line adjustment located just forward of the main lever. Turning this adjustment presets the main lever in the open position, allowing paint to flow as soon as the main lever is depressed. The thread count on both of these adjustments is extremely fine, allowing the user to accurately regulate the flow through the airbrush.

Airbrushes without this control can still be set up as single-action airbrushes. By loosening the needle chuck, retracting the needle slightly, then retightening the needle chuck, the airbrush will now operate as a single-action. Setting the flow in this manner is not as precise as with the dedicated control, but the results can be very similar.

Certain models in the Aztek line offer a single-action adjustment, too. The rolling knob in the back of

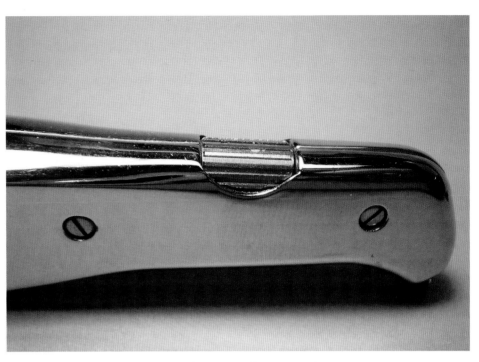

Aztek 777 single-action adjustment.

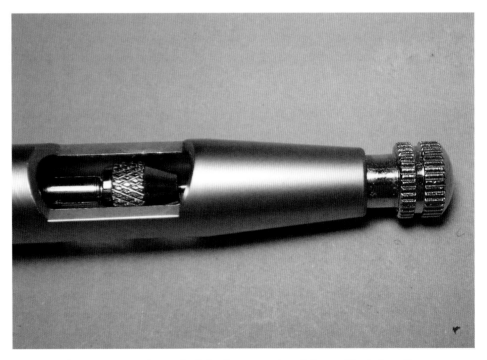

Preset adjustment on the end of the PrecisionAire Master Treo's handle.

47

Richpen 303C with color cup horizontal .

Richpen 303C with color cup vertical.

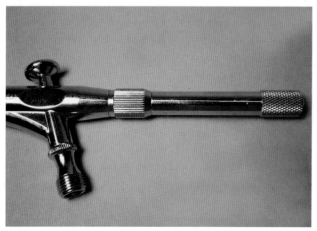

Richpen 033G single-action flow control.

the body can be set to allow the flow of paint similar to a single-action airbrush.

A preset adjustment is located on the handle of some airbrushes. This restricts the backward motion of the main lever to the point that is chosen by the operator. Once set, the main lever can be pulled all the way back, ensuring the same amount of paint flow each time. This adjustment can be very helpful when spraying a consistent, repeating pattern. Limiting the main lever movement ensures application of the same amount of paint each time. The preset handle may also act as a safety net to ensure the main lever can't be fully opened. This will prevent the main lever from being accidentally pulled back and dispensing paint everywhere.

Preset handles are an interesting option. Artists who learned on airbrushes without this adjustment rarely use the preset handle, while a user who is starting from scratch may find the adjustment quite useful.

Side-feed airbrushes offer the user a very unique ability. Most gravity-feed airbrushes cannot operate vertically due to the backward angle of the color cup. Tipping them backward beyond a certain point will allow the paint to spill from the cup or leak from the breather hole. Because the side-feed cup is held in place by friction, the cup itself can be rotated front to back, allowing the airbrush to operate at any angle. The Richpen Phoenix 303C is a good example of a side-feed airbrush with a rotating color cup.

Dedicated-single-action airbrushes can have their flow controls in different parts of the body, depending on how they are set up. The paint flow adjuster on such internal-mix single-action airbrushes as the Richpen 013G and the Fengda BD-206 is integrated into the handle of the airbrush. As the handle is rotated, fine threads will move the needle in and out according to the desired paint flow. On external-mix airbrushes such as the Paasche H model, the paint and air converge at the head of the airbrush. The needle assembly of Paasche H allows the user to rotate the outer assembly. As this outer assembly is rotated the housing moves up or down on the needle allowing

Paasche H head assembly.

Paasche H needle in the fully closed position.

Paasche H needle in the fully open position.

control over exactly how much paint is allowed into the flow of air.

These adjustments can take many different forms, depending on how the manufacture of the specific airbrush has evolved. Despite their cosmetic differences, their functions are the same. Take a moment before using any new airbrush and look over the instruction manual to see what adjustments are available on your new airbrush, and how to adjust them to get the most performance out of it.

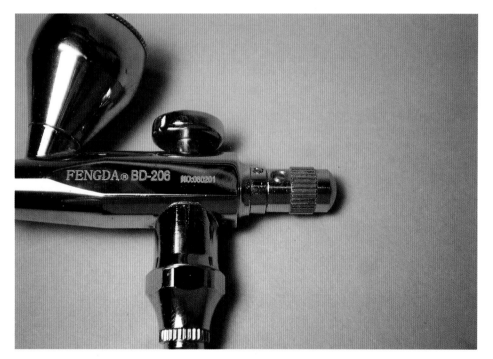

Fengda BD-206 single-action flow control.

Chapter Eight

Airbrush Bodies

The Foundation On Which Each Airbrush Is Built

The body of any airbrush is its foundation. Nearly all of the tool's ergonomics are based on this part. The internal actions of the components are often governed by how they are secured to the body. Even ease of cleaning and maintenance can be influenced by how the body of an airbrush is designed.

Nickel, with chrome-plated brass construction comprise the majority of airbrushes on the market today, but a few exceptions exist - such as the Aztek 470 and the Badger 350. Both of these airbrushes use a composite material in the manufacture of their bodies.

Considering the manufacturing processes are

Nearly imperceptible weld joint on an expensive airbrush.

very similar regardless of the brand, it usually is very easy to see the quality in the way an airbrush is constructed. For example, look carefully at the weld joints. With a quality airbrush these joints will be clean and even. In a poorly manufactured airbrush the welds will be obvious and inconsistent. Look for these welds near the base of the color cup of a gravity-feed airbrush. On a siphon-feed, look at where the air valve enters the body. Both of these spots are very visible, and will quickly indicate the quality of airbrush you are looking at.

Less carefully welded joint of an inexpensive airbrush.

Features of the body of the airbrush largely determine the comfort in the way it fits in your hand. Overall shape and size are the first characteristics that you should look at. Some airbrushes, the Paasche VL and the Badger Crescendo, for example, have large oversized bodies that resemble fountain pens. The advantage of this style of airbrush is that in some hands, the larger size can reduce fatigue. This is one of the reasons the Paasche VL is one of the most popular airbrushes for T-shirt artists. Its large, comfortable body makes it easier to paint with for long periods of time.

Recently, the trend for smaller bodied airbrushes has begun to pick up speed. Airbrushes with thinner bodies - such as the Iwata HP-BCS, Vega 2000 and the Paasche Millennium - offer an alternative to the bigger bodied airbrushes, while giving the same over

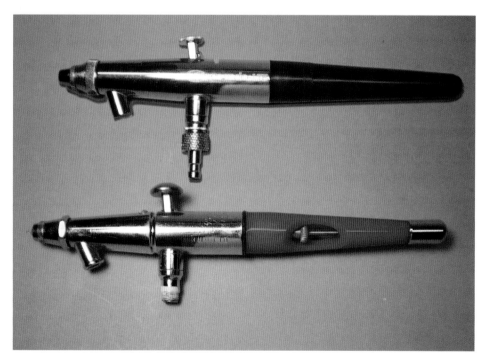

Top: Badger Crescendo
Bottom: Paasche VL

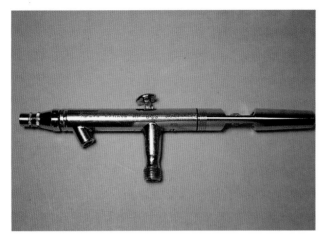

Iwata Eclipse BCS.

Collar of the Sotar 20/20.

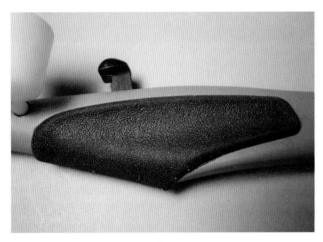

Comfort grips of the Aztek 470.

Slotted color cup of the Peak C5.

Side cut outs of the Richpen 213C.

Funnel color cup of the Iwata HP-CH.

all performance. Until this point, the majority of the smaller bodied airbrushes were designed for fine atomization with thinner paint.

Consequently, the size of the body of the airbrush becomes your own personal choice. The feel of the brush in your hand, in many instances, will really be the only difference. The Paasche VL and Millennium are the perfect examples. One has the large, fountain pen style body and the other is the smaller, ballpoint pen style, yet they share exactly the same internal components.

Airbrush manufacturers have taken different routes in body designs to add comfort to the use of their products. With the Sotar 20/20, a scalloped collar is installed around the top of the air valve body to give the operator a better grip. Testors created large rubber pads to make the body of the Aztek 470 more comfortable and to aid in grip. In the Richpen 213 and others, the ergonomics are machined directly into the body of the brush. The sides of the Phoenix airbrush body are flattened to give superior grip.

The design of the components of the airbrush body is not limited to ergonomics. Function plays a large role in the design of a quality airbrush. For instance, in a gravity-feed airbrush, the shape and style of the color cup can have a great impact on the way the brush functions. The Peak C-5 has a small slotted reservoir at the bottom of the color cup while the Iwata HP-C Plus has a more funnel-shaped design. A scallop taken from the back edge

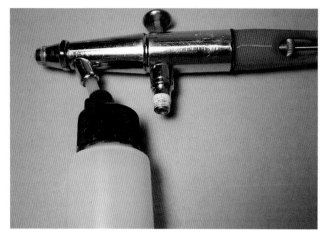

Same bottle assembly fits on the Paasche VL.

One piece air valve housing of the Iwata Eclipse CS

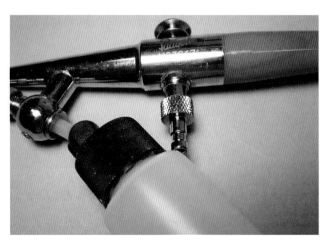

Incorrect bottle assembly interferes with the air valve of the Paasche H.

Removable air valve housing of the Sogolee V6000.

Cleaning Chamber for the Peak X-5.

Female threads on the Iwata Custom Micron handle.

of the Iwata Custom Micron B's color cup gives the operator's finger more room.

For siphon-feed airbrushes, this attention to form and function plays a large role as well. The feed stem on the top of the paint jar of Paasche's "H" model is at a lesser angle than on its "VL" model. This simple change in angle ensures that the bottle assembly does not interfere with the air valve assembly.

How the air valve housing is manufactured on the body of the airbrush plays a role in its operation. In such models as the Iwata HP-BCS, the air valve body is welded to the main body, while the air valve body can be completely unscrewed from the Iwata HP-C Plus. The latter design makes it very easy to get inside the airbrush body for cleaning.

The Iwata HP-BC, Peak X5, and others have small cleaning chambers on the top of the airbrush that, when removed, allow a cleaning brush to be passed through, making maintenance extremely easy.

Custom aftermarket parts are becoming more common so it is important to be familiar with the construction of your airbrush. Then you can be certain that the new parts will function properly. Something as simple as how the handle of the airbrush threads onto the body can make a difference. In some airbrushes the handle has the male threads and in other instances the body has the male threads. Careful inspection of your air brush will ensure that you always get the correct parts.

Other small, inconspicuous parts also play a major role in the function of the airbrush. For example, a small setscrew is located in the bottom of the body in most airbrushes. This tiny screw's only function is to prevent the needle guide from spinning inside the body of the airbrush. If this screw is over tightened, it will cause the trigger and needle assembly to bind, and not move forward and back.

Understanding what ergonomic features are important to you will have a tremendous impact on how an airbrush performs for you. Even the most refined, expensive airbrush can cause fatigue, and will ultimately discourage you if it is uncomfortable in your hand. After purchasing your new airbrush, take the time to really get to know and understand its construction and design. With a working knowledge of the different aspects of the body of the airbrush, you can quickly resolve any problems that may arise.

Male threads on the Peak X5 handle.

Setscrew on the bottom of the Iwata Custom Micron SB.

Chapter Nine

Care and Maintenance

Important Steps

Even well designed and sturdily manufactured airbrushes will soon fail if their care and maintenance are ignored. The cleaning procedures described here will prevent many problems.

Still, accidents or other problems can occur, and you may need to "go in" to remove dried paint or replace worn or damaged parts. The following sequences describe the disassembly and repair of several popular airbrushes. If your airbrush is not illustrated, at least one of those pictured should be a typical example that you can use as a guide.

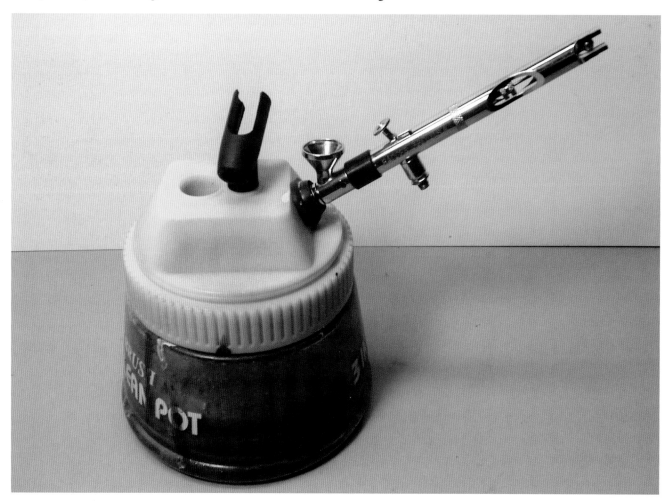

Container for waste

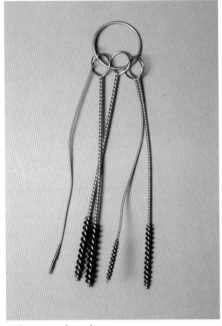
Cleaning brushes

Squirt bottle

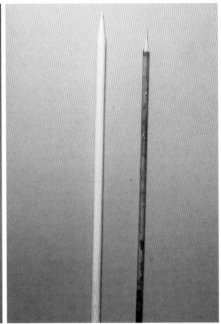
Bamboo meat skewers

BEFORE YOU BEGIN

Here is a list of tools and supplies that make taking care of your airbrush very easy.

Cleaning brushes - Having several different sizes of cleaning brushes ensures that you can quickly and completely remove stubborn material from any of the passageways of the airbrush.

Squirt Bottle
Receptacle - for used paint
Bamboo meat skewers - These are amazingly strong and can be used to safely remove dried paint from the inside of the tip of the airbrush.

Airbrush cleaner - Having the correct cleaner to match the type of paint that you are using can make all the difference in the world.

Airbrush lube - While a clean, well-maintained airbrush does not require any lubrication, using this non-reactive lubricant can cut down on wear and tear to the airbrush.

Wet and dry sandpaper - 600, 1500 and 2000 grit sandpaper can be used while straightening and polishing bent needles.

Non-silicon metal polish - Fine-grit metal polish can also be used in final stages of needle repair.

Suede scrap - Suede is a perfect surface on which to polish metal.

1x1x4-inch oak block - This small hardwood block is used as a surface for straightening bent needles.

Sharpening stone - a good quality sharpening stone, judiciously applied, can make the difference in the performance of the needle.

Tweezers - A good set of fine point tweezers are invaluable for getting hard to reach pieces in place.

Beeswax - This natural sealant is perfect for restoring air tight seals

Nozzle wrenches - When the airbrush has a threaded nozzle it should come with a matching wrench to remove it. The nozzle is extremely delicate so make sure that you have the correct wrench to avoid damage.

Needle-nose pliers - Any type of pliers can do massive damage to the soft metals of an airbrush, yet the careful use of a good set of needle nosed pliers can help to remove a stubborn needle.

Oil paint bristle brush - A good quality, stiff bristle, oil painting brush is perfect for quick cleanouts as well as being extremely durable.

Paper towels - Good quality paper towels make a great, soft and absorbent work surface.

Airbrush cleaners

Airbrush lube

Cleaning dish and paper towels.

Small bowl - A small clear glass bowl is valuable for soaking small parts, and being able to see through it will allow you to pick it up and see where those pieces are without having to fish for them.

PROPER WORKSPACE

The first and primary rule here is never clean your airbrushes over a sink. As tempting as it is, the chance is far too great to slip and lose an expensive piece down the drain.

The best place to work on your airbrush is on a large, clean and flat table with good lighting. I generally spread some paper towels across the area that I plan to work on. The paper towels prevent small dropped parts from bouncing off the table, and will also absorb any excess cleaner that remains on the parts.

DISASSEMBLY OF VARIOUS STYLES OF AIRBRUSHES

In this section we will look at the general disassembly of several different styles of airbrushes. While all of these operate on the same principles, each company tends to design and manufacture their products in slightly different ways. If your particular airbrush is not covered here, you should be able to find and follow on a similar model.

Wet/dry sandpaper and suede fabric.

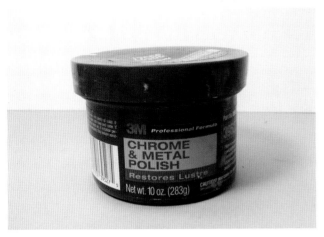

Non-silicone metal polish

Beeswax

Sharpening stone and block of oak

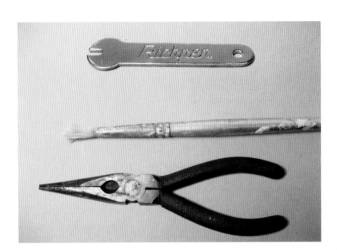

From top to bottom: nozzle wrench, oil paint brush, Needle-nose pliers.

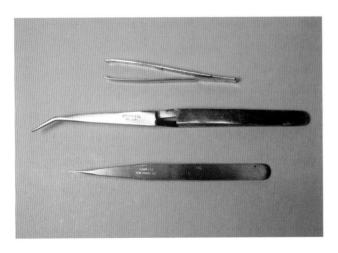

Tweezers

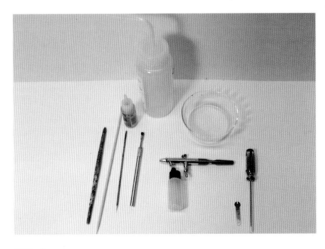

Workspace

RICHPEN 213 DISASSEMBLY

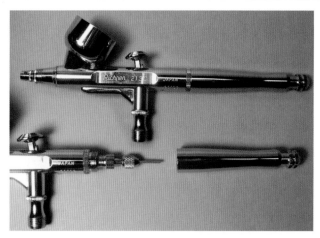

1. Top: Richpen 213C double-action, gravity-feed air-brush. Bottom: Unscrew handle from back of brush.

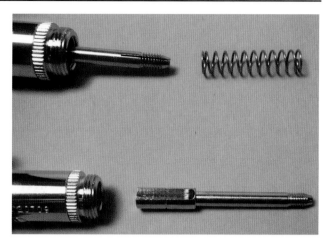

4. Top: Remove needle spring. Bottom: Remove needle guide.

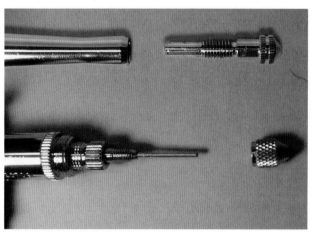

2. Top: Unscrew preset adjustment. Bottom: Loosen and remove needle chuck.

5. Remove main lever.

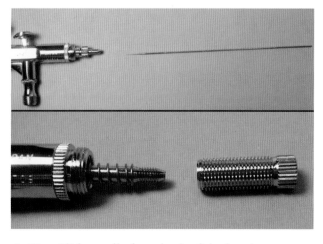

3. Top: Slide needle from back of the brush. Bottom: Unscrew needle-adjusting sleeve.

6. Remove auxiliary lever.

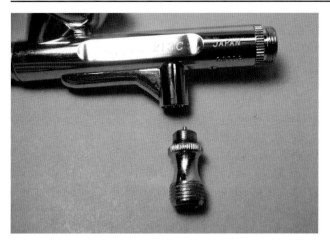

7. Unscrew air valve.

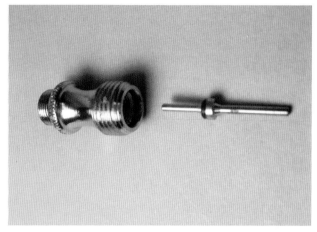

10. Remove air valve. It's easy to damage the air piston O-ring. Carefully remove with tweezers.

8. Unscrew air valve nut. Caution: this nut has a tensioned spring that will shoot out as it is being loosened.

11. Remove air valve washer. Remove Teflon needle seal per instructions later in this chapter.

9. Remove air valve spring.

12. Remove needle cap.

13. Remove nozzle cap.

14. Remove nozzle. Use supplied wrench to loosen, then unscrew with fingers. The nozzle is very delicate.

PAASCHE VL AIRBRUSH

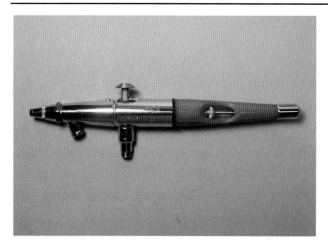

1. Paasche VL double-action, siphon-feed airbrush.

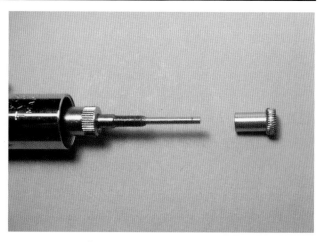

3. Loosen and remove locknut.

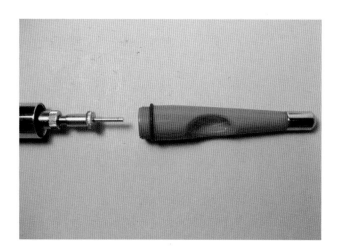

2. Remove handle.

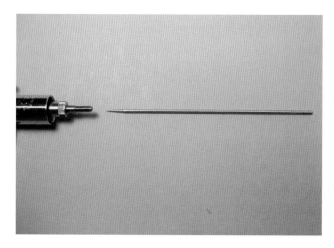

4. Remove needle.

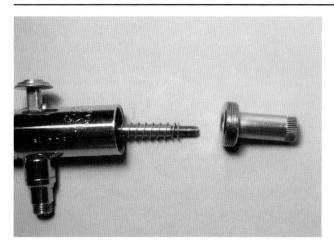

5. Unscrew and remove needle-adjusting sleeve.

8. Unscrew air valve nut - as with all airbrushes, be aware of the spring tension behind this piece.

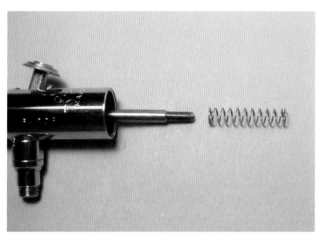

6. Remove spring.

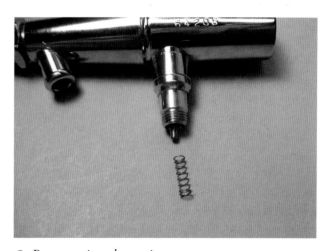

9. Remove air valve spring.

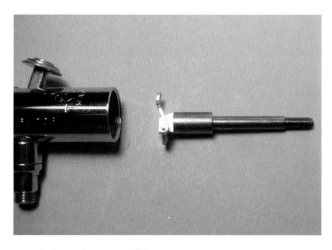

7. Slide rocker assembly out.

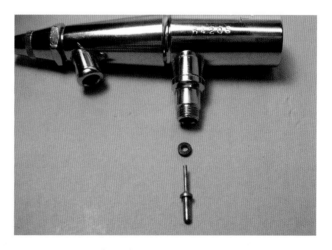

10. Remove valve plunger.

11. Unscrew air cap.

12. Unscrew air cap body. Reverse the process to reassemble.

DeVilbiss DAGR Airbrush

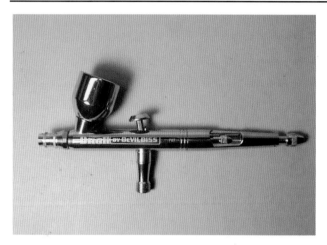

1. DeVilbiss DAGR double-action, gravity-feed airbrush.

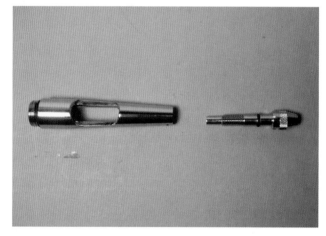

3. Unscrew preset adjustment.

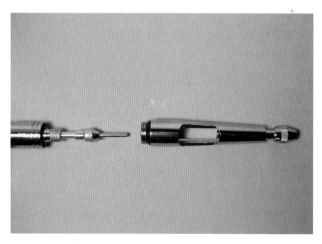

2. Unscrew handle from back of brush.

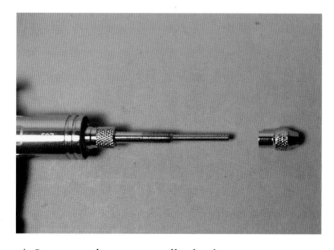

4. Loosen and remove needle chuck.

DeVilbiss DAGR CONTINUED

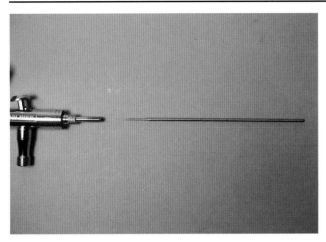

5. Slide needle from back of the brush.

8. Remove needle guide.

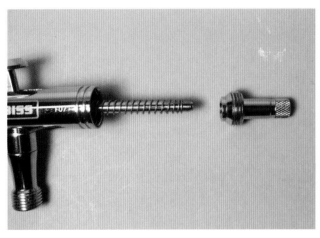

6. Unscrew needle-adjusting sleeve.

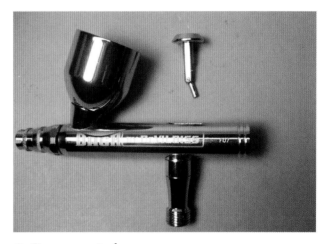

9. Remove main lever.

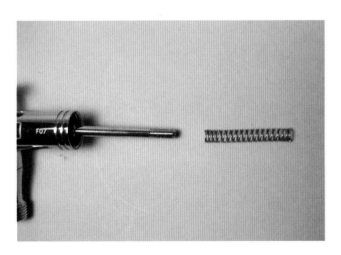

7. Remove needle spring.

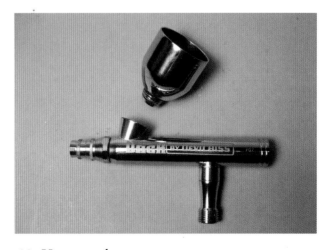

10. Unscrew color cup.

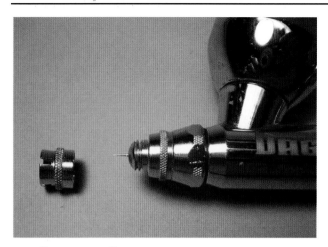

12. *Remove needle cap.*

14. *Remove air cap.*

13. *Remove nozzle cap.*

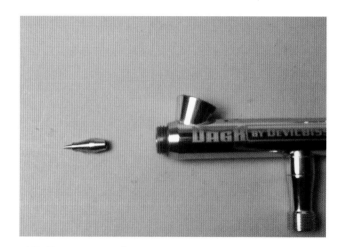

15. *Remove nozzle.*

Types of Cleaners

The list of airbrush cleaners is long. The main thing to remember is to look for cleaners that match the type of paint you are using.

Water-based paints such as watercolors, gouache, fabric paint and so forth, have similar water-based cleaners. Some are concentrated while others are ready to use out of the bottle. Household cleaners often work well as a cleaner for water-based paint, but products containing ammonia should be avoided. Ammonia, espe-cially mixed with water, is corrosive to the inside of an airbrush.

Automotive urethanes can be cleaned with the same products used to reduce them, yet a more cost effective cleaner for this type of paint is simply lacquer thinner.

Temporary tattoo paint and tanning solu-tion cleans up very well with isopropyl alcohol

Food coloring cleans up with a highly dilut-ed mixture of dish soap and water.

SOGOLEE 6000 AIRBRUSH

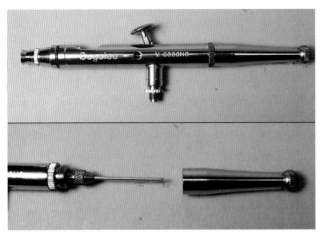

1. Top: Sogolee 6000 double-action, gravity-feed air-brush. Bottom: Unscrew handle from back of brush.

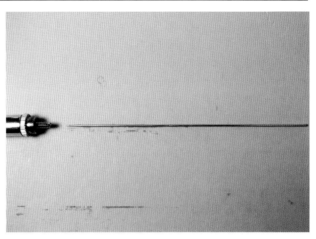

4. Slide needle from back of the brush.

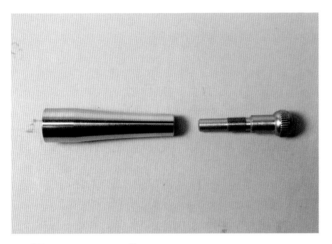

2. Unscrew preset adjustment.

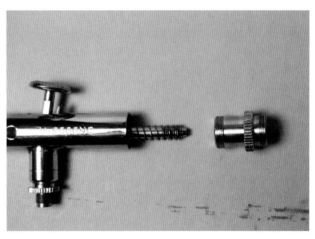

5. Unscrew needle-adjusting sleeve.

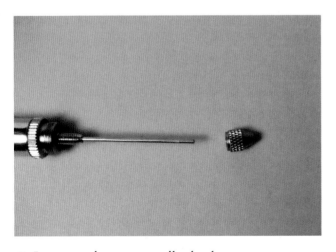

3. Loosen and remove needle chuck.

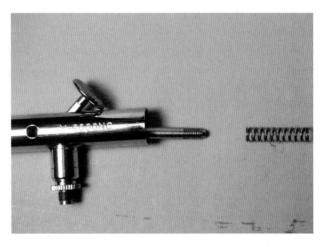

6. Remove needle spring.

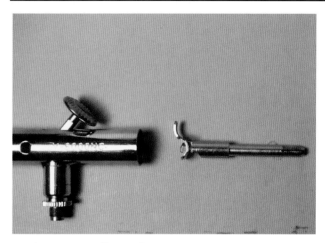

7. Remove needle guide.

10. Remove air cap.

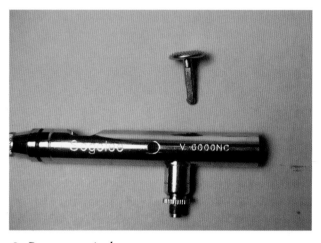

8. Remove main lever.

11. Remove nozzle.

9. Remove needle cap.

12. Remove nozzle. Reverse the process to reassemble.

VEGA OMNI 3000 AIRBRUSH

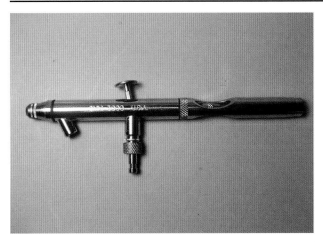

1. Vega Omni 3000 double-action, siphon-feed

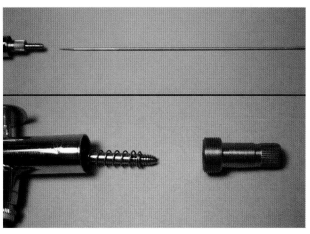

4. Top: Slide needle from back of the brush.
Bottom: Unscrew needle-adjusting sleeve.

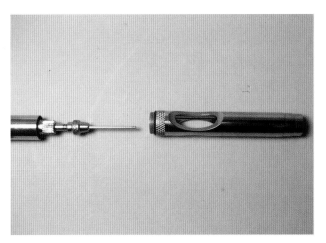

2. Unscrew handle from back of brush.

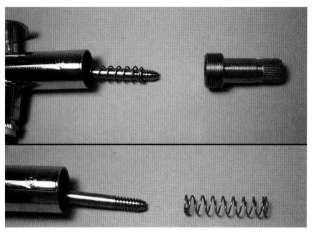

5. Top: Unscrew needle-adjusting sleeve.
Bottom: Remove needle spring.

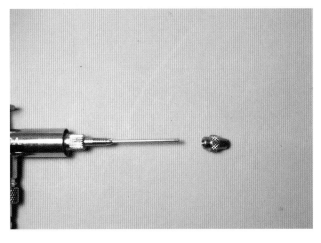

3. Loosen and remove needle chuck.

6. Remove needle guide.

VEGA OMNI 3000 CONTINUED

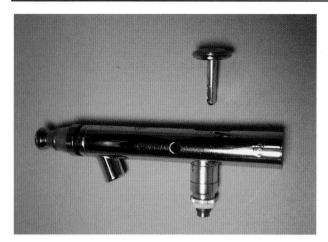

7. *Remove main lever.*

10. *Remove nozzle.*

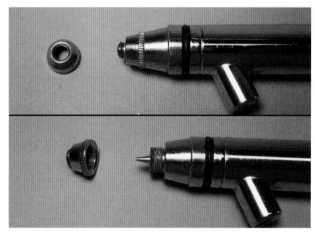

8. *Top: Remove needle cap.*
Bottom: Remove nozzle cap.

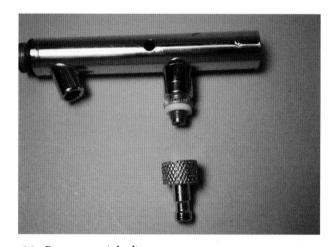

11. *Remove quick-disconnect.*

9. *Remove air cap.*

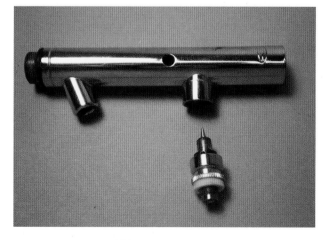

12. *Remove air valve. Reverse the process to reassemble.*

CLEANING - GRAVITY-FEED FLUSH

1. Pour back unused paint

2. Wipe out excess paint

3. Brush out any remaining paint with cleaner

HOW TO CLEAN

GRAVITY-FEED FLUSH

Simple color flush of gravity-feed, and side-feed brushes.

Remove as much paint as possible from the color cup. If it is a pure unmixed color, return as much as you can to the original paint container.

Clean residual paint out of the cup with cleaner.

Spray straight cleaner through the airbrush.

Your airbrush is now ready for the next color.

4. Spray cleaner through brush

CLEANING - SIPHON FLUSH OUT

Flush out excess paint

Spray cleaner from bottle

SIPHON CLEANING

Simple color flush of siphon-feed airbrushes
Remove paint bottle and flush out paint stem with cleaner.

Attach bottle with cleaner to brush and spray until clear.

Airbrush is now ready for the next color.

END OF THE DAY CLEANING

The process for the end of the day cleaning is nearly identical to the color flush. The only addition would be to add one or two additional flush outs with the clear cleaner to ensure that there is no residual paint in the brush to dry and harden.

Siphon feed airbrushes are airtight with the exception of the small breather hole at the top of the bottle assembly. By covering this hole, the paint bottle may be left on the brush without fear of things drying up inside the airbrush.

One very important note in cleaning your airbrush; identify any toxins in the waste you are producing as a byproduct of your work, and be certain to discard the waste in an appropriate manner. Pouring toxic chemicals down a sink can be disastrous to the environment.

COMMON REPAIRS

Straightening a bent needle

Accidents with the needle are a common occurrence. The super fine tip can be bent with a slight touch. Having extra needles and nozzles on hand is always a good idea, yet the time will come when you will be down to your last one.

Before removing the bent needle carefully inspect it to see how bad the damage is. In the first picture the needle is only slightly bent and can be safely removed from the airbrush

In the second picture the needle is badly damaged and trying to remove this needle will cause additional damage to the nozzle. In this instance you can gently bend the needle back so that it is straight enough to safely remove from the airbrush.

Once the needle is removed you can continue to straighten it to the point you will be able to get by until you can replace it with a new one, or sharpen it to completely repair it.

The tools you need to straighten the needle are the wrench that was supplied with the airbrush and a small hardwood block. The first step is to rest the tip of the needle on the block of wood at the angle of the original taper of the needle. Next, place the wrench on top of the

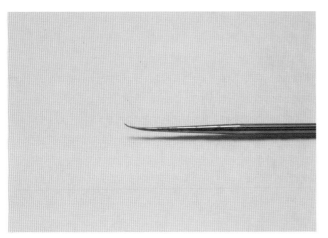

Bent needle

Needle straight enough to remove

Bent needle in airbrush

Positioning needle on oak block

Straightening needle with finger nails

Pressing with wrench while rolling needle

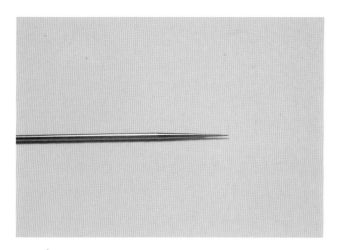

Straightened needle

Applying beeswax

Soak end of airbrush in compatible cleaner (see text).

needle and begin applying pressure to the wrench while rolling it back and forth. The combination of the pressure you apply to the wrench, and the rolling action, will remove the major bends in the needle.

This method will return the needle to usable condition. You will not be able to produce the fine atomization or have the control you would with a new needle, but it will function enough to get you through.

Sealing threads

The airbrush relies on certain parts to be completely airtight. If the air cap, for instance, is not sealed the vacuum that would normally be created is compromised and the airbrush will not produce a constant pressure to atomize paint. It will skip as it sprays. It is very similar to trying to drink from a straw with a hole in it.

Common beeswax is an excellent, non reactive sealant that can be used throughout the airbrush. Applying it is very simple. Take a small amount of wax on a bamboo meat skewer and apply it directly to the threads. Twist the threads with your fingers, and the heat from your fingers will soften the wax into the threads evenly.

The parts of the airbrush that should be waxed are the threads on the nozzle, head cap and air cap. It is unnecessary to wax the needle cap. The threads in the air valve do not need waxing either, due to the rubber seals that are already in place.

Removing broken nozzle threads

Occasionally, while installing or removing a nozzle the nozzle will break off leaving the threads in the airbrush. Removal of these broken threads is simple.

First soak the end of the airbrush in the appropriate cleaner for the paint you were using. It is important to soften any residual paint that might have dried on the broken threads. Dried paint acts just like glue.

Once any paint is softened, you can push the sharp end of a bamboo meat skewer firmly into the opening where the threads are, and steadily unscrew the broken threads. The nice thing about this method is that you can't damage the threads in the airbrush with the skewer.

If a harder object, such as a jeweler's file or small knife blade is used to remove the threads, you run the risk of seriously damaging the threads in the body of the airbrush. If these threads are damaged the airbrush will no longer function.

Fixing a sticky main lever

Identifying the causes of this common problems is at the top of your list in making your airbrush experience effortless and fun. One way to achieve this is to understand what some problems have in common.

If any part of your airbrush seems sticky or sluggish then you can be sure there is dirt or paint where you don't want it. The open slot at the top of the airbrush from which the main lever extends is a classic trap for dirt, dust and stray paint. Once that paint gets into the body of the brush and dries, especially near the air valve pin, it can cause all kinds of problems.

Your first job is to clean out the brush as if you were doing a color change.

Second, remove the handle and all the internal parts from the main body of the airbrush. This includes unscrewing the air valve from the bottom of the airbrush. You do not need to take apart the air valve yet, it is a sealed system and it is unlikely anything has gotten inside.

Third is to use the cleaning brushes with cleaner and scrub out the entire body of the airbrush.

Next, wipe off the air valve pin.

Reassemble the airbrush and it should work like new. If it does not, then the problem could be in the air valve itself. The O-ring in the air valve is usually not solvent-proof and can be damaged when exposed to solvents. Replacing this O-ring at this point would solve the problem.

Insert meat skewer.

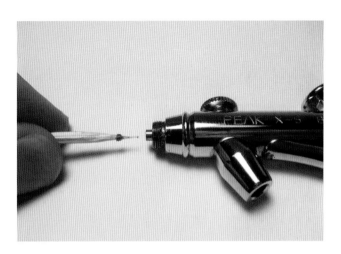

Unscrew broken threads

Remove air valve.

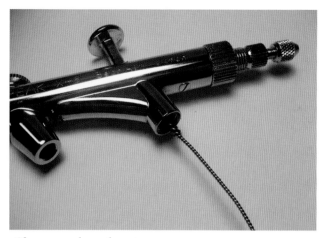

Clean out the valve pin passageway.

Clean out the body of the brush.

REMOVING THE TEFLON NEEDLE SEAL

Some airbrushes have a removable seal in the body that stops paint from flowing backwards into the body of the airbrush. While the need to remove the seal is rare, it is a good idea to know where it is and how to replace it if the need does arise. The nut that holds this seal in place usually has a slot in which a long thin screwdriver will fit. Gently loosen the nut and remove it.

REPLACING THE TEFLON PACKING SET

Slide the packing set on the needle of the airbrush. Holding the airbrush nose down, slide the needle into the back of the airbrush and the packing set will slide into the right position. Again, be very gentle when using the screwdriver. If you meet even the slightest resistance, stop, unscrew it and realign the threads. Crosstreading this piece in the airbrush will ruin the body of the brush.

When replacing the nozzle, again thread it completely on with your fingers. You cannot strip the threads on the body, or the nozzle, if you only use your fingers. The wrench can be used at the very end to apply extremely soft pressure to make certain it is secure.

Wipe off the valve pin.

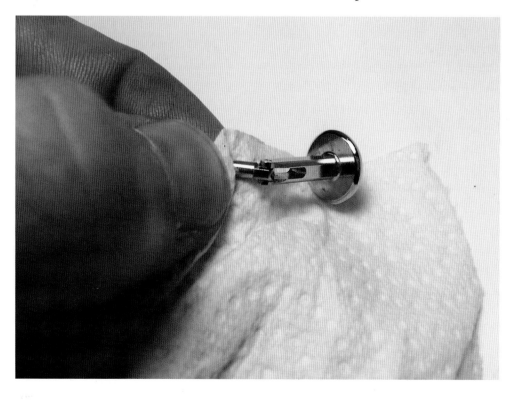

sive air lines that are designed to move low air pressures will likely rupture if higher pressures are put through them. This rupture will often occur near one of the fittings, either near the airbrush or near the compressor.

Vinyl air lines are flexible, thin and light. These smaller hoses are intended for use in low-pressure applications such as makeup and fingernail painting, scale modeling and temporary tattoos. The common color for these hoses is black although they are available in a clear vinyl as well. This clear material allows the operator to see any moisture that is traveling through the lines.

Because of the flexibility in the manufacture of vinyl, these hoses can also be made to retain a tight coil shape. The coiled line allows a long length of hose to take up a small amount of space.

The disadvantage of these coiled hoses is that if more than one is used, they can easily become tangled with each other. The advantage is clearly seen in the compact way that the hose returns to its coiled form. The compact shape of the coiled hose also helps to keep the hose retracted away from the wok area.

Braided hoses are made of rubber tubing wrapped with braided cloth. These hoses are deigned to deliver a higher pressure and will generally withstand more wear and tear. Also, the fittings on these hoses are usually crimped into place making them very durable. The braiding on these

hoses is available in different colors, which allows the operator to color code the airbrushes by the airlines.

The length of a hose can have varying effects on the way the airbrush operates. Obviously the working conditions should be the first thing to consider when choosing the length of the air line. In an instance where the artist is very close to the manifold or compressor a shorter hose helps to keep things from getting tangled.

T-shirt artists are an excellent example of this. A standard T-shirt station will have eight to 12 airbrushes, each with a different color paint in them. The artists' profit is determined by how fast they are able to produce a shirt. With that many airbrushes being exchanged quickly, short four foot hoses attached to a manifold on the easel keep things well organized and tangle free. On the other hand an artist who primarily does interior wall murals would never be able to function with a short four-foot hose. Air lines for this application can be as long as 25 feet.

Straight vinyl air hose.

Coiled vinyl air hose.

The length of the hose can have a direct impact on the performance of both the compressor and the airbrush. A long air line allows the air plenty of time and distance to cool as it travels. The moisture in this cooled air re-condenses and is easily caught if a moisture trap is installed near the airbrush. The disadvantage to using a longer air line is that a stronger compressor is required to keep that length of hose pressurized. A small single piston compressor will have difficulty keeping up with a hose more than 10 feet long.

Connecting the airbrush to the compressor can be done in several different ways. The standard threaded fitting will supply the proper connection between the airbrush and the compressor, yet other connectors will allow quicker change outs. Quick-connect fittings allow the user to quickly change one hose between different airbrushes. The connection is a simple valve that allows air to pass once it is connected, but instantly blocks the air when the airbrush is removed. The quick-connect hose has a special fitting on one end with a non-threaded valve. A male coupling

Braided air hose.

is attached to the air-brush. This coupling clicks firmly into the quick-connect valve on the hose.

Quick-connect fittings have several advantages over standard threaded hoses. First is the complete ease with which airbrushes can be swapped out, back and forth. While the threads on the fittings are air-brush brand specific, the male couplings that connect to the hose are the same. This neat feature allows you to use multiple brands of airbrushes with the very same air hose.

The quick-connect fitting also eliminates the need to lower the air pressure before removing the airbrush. These types of hoses generally come in 10 and 20 foot lengths.

Quick-connect fittings are also available for attachment to standard hoses. There are two types of these add-on fittings. The first type screws onto the hose's standard threaded fitting, while the second type requires you to cut off the old threaded fitting and replace it with the new quick-connect fitting.

Moisture traps located on the hose or at the airbrush have become a popular option. Three small filters act as a last bit of insurance against any moisture that has

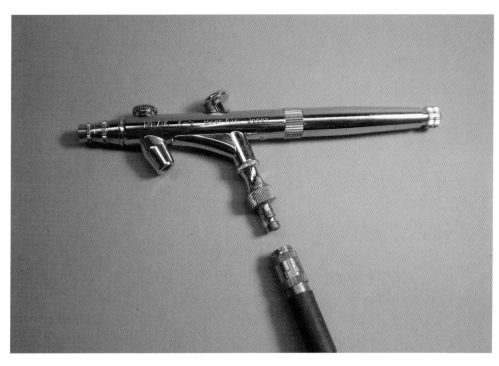

Pre-installed quick-connect fitting.

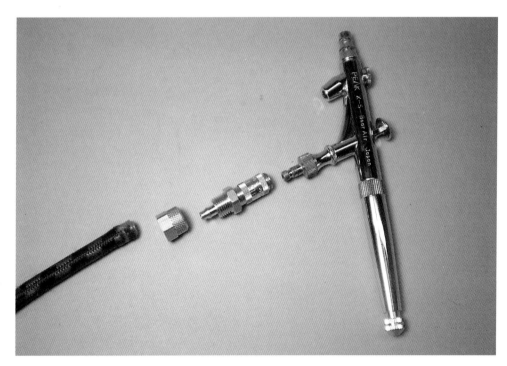

Clamp on type quick-connect.

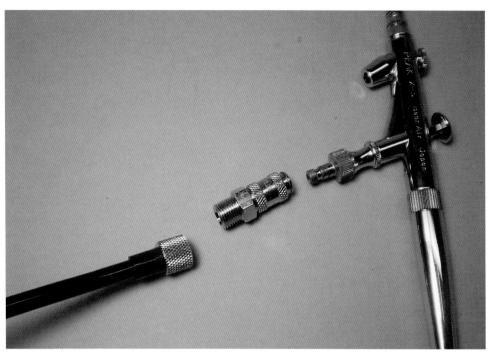

Screw on type quick connect.

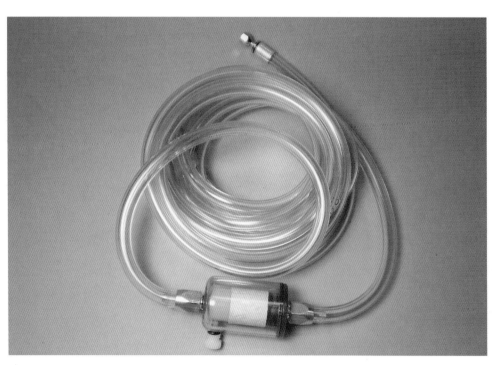

Factory installed air line moisture trap.

made it past the larger trap on the compressor.

These small moisture traps, while effective, will not solve the problem of excessive moisture coming through the lines. If that is happening you need to turn your attention back to the compressor and the demand you are putting on it.

As with the quick-connect fittings, the in line moisture traps are offered preinstalled in the hose, or can be purchased separately and added to an existing hose. The moisture traps that you install yourself generally come in two different styles. The first involves cutting the hose near the airbrush end and clamping the trap in place. The second type screws directly onto the airbrush and has threads to attach the hose to it.

While a quick-connect fitting allows instant changes between multiple airbrushes, you may find the need to have several airbrushes hooked up and ready to go at any time. This can be done with a multiple-port manifold. These manifolds allow the user to attach many airbrushes simultaneously to the same compressor. Keep in mind that merely having several airbrushes hooked up to the same compressor does not put additional strain on the compressor. However, having several people using airbrushes at the same time while connected to the same compressor will.

One reason to have multiple airbrushes attached simultaneously is to allow rapid color changes. T-shirt artists provide the best example of this advantage. In that situation, time is money and the faster they can produce a shirt the more money they make. Having all the colors available at your fingertips, ready to go, is a tremendous time saver.

Manifolds for a compressor can be anything from a simple T-valve made up of standard plumbing fittings to the commercially available multi-port units. Try to imagine your future needs when choosing a manifold to avoid having to purchase a larger one later.

Finally, as with just about every connection on your airbrush system, making sure that those fittings are airtight is important. This holds especially true with a manifold that has the potential to leak a great deal of air, given the number of hoses connected to it. Simply wrapping all the threads with plumbers' Teflon tape before making the connections will ensure an airtight system.

Clamp on type moisture trap.

Airbrush manifolds.

Chapter Thirteen

Beyond the Basics

Fine Tune Your Airbrush

Today's airbrushes are made to exacting specifications with levels of tooling precision that have never been reached before. Modern airbrushes atomize paint more finely while allowing more control and requiring less maintenance than their older cousins. Airbrushes today are extremely refined, yet limitations imposed by the cost of manufacturing open the door for the individual user to custom-tune their own airbrushes for even better performance.

Custom-ground trigger pad on a Richpen Phoenix 213C.

These performance improvements often result from a few simple steps. However, before making any modifications to your airbrush, understand that taking these actions will often result in the voiding of the manufacturer's warranty. It is always best to check with the manufacturer before undertaking any changes to your airbrush.

MODIFYING THE NEEDLE

Modern methods of manufacturing airbrush needles leave tiny score marks on the taper of the needle. These microscopic ridges attract and hold paint increasing the amount of tip dry - the material (paint) that is deposited on the exposed end of the airbrush needle during normal operation. If not periodically removed this collected dry material will restrict the flow of air and paint. By removing these ridges the paint will flow more smoothly off the needle and acquire tip dry less frequently. The process for polishing the needle is relatively simple and only takes a few minutes.

This polishing works very well on new needles, yet it can also be used as the final steps after straightening a bent needle. The first step is to remove the score marks from the taper of the needle. Wrap a piece of 2000 grit wet/dry sandpaper over a small block of hard wood. Put a few drops of water or light oil on the paper, then place the tip of the needle on the paper so the entire length of the taper makes complete contact. Lightly draw the needle toward you while rolling it between your fingers. It is easy to tell if the entire taper is making contact with the paper by the trail it leaves behind in the oil or water.

Use caution to ensure that the entire taper is making contact throughout the whole motion. Changing the angle at which the needle is being held will change the taper of the needle and may adversely affect the airbrush's performance. A shorter taper offers better paint flow but with lesser atomization; a longer taper offers finer atomization with a higher accumulation of tip dry.

Once you have made several passes on the 2000 grit paper, the taper of the needle should be evenly scuffed up. Replace the sandpaper with a small piece of suede on the block of wood. Apply a very small amount of non-silicone polishing compound to the suede. Holding the needle at the same angle with the taper making complete contact, begin pulling it toward you through the polishing compound, rolling the needle in your fingers at the same time. Repeat this process several times and the residual polish on the suede will begin to turn black as small amounts of metal are polished off the needle. Periodically wipe the needle clean and take a look at your progress. The goal is for the taper of the needle to have a mirror finish.

The use of a magnifying glass or a jeweler's loupe is very helpful to get a really good look at your progress in the polishing process.

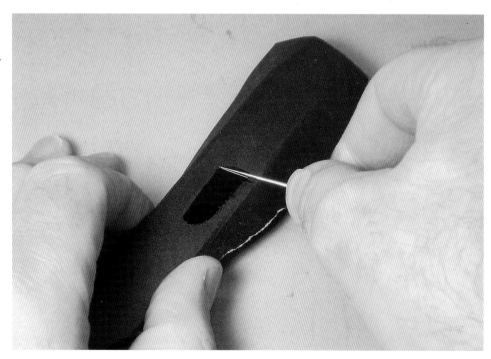

Gently drag the taper of the needle across 2000-grit sandpaper on a block of wood.

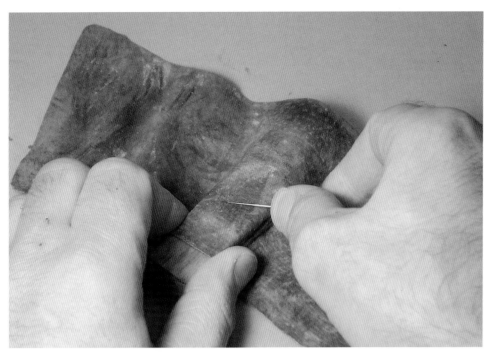

Polish the taper of the needle using suede and rubbing compound.

Polishing the needle in this way has a big impact on very small, detail oriented airbrushes. Because working with details often involves more air than paint, tip dry is much more common, than when pure paint flow is desired. Polishing a needle on a larger nozzle airbrush will improve its performance slightly, but the benefits probably would not outweigh the effort expended to do the modification.

Some manufacturers, such as Paasche Airbrush Company, offer pre-polished needles. These factory polished needles can save you the time it would take to polish your own.

MODIFYING THE NOZZLE

Just as the needle has machining marks, so does the nozzle. In the case of the nozzle however, these small ridges do not collect paint, rather they can minutely alter the flow of air across the nozzle. Most of these tiny ridges can also be polished off. A word of caution here - changes to the needle may affect the performance of the airbrush slightly. Changes to the opening of the nozzle will have a drastic effect on the performance, and usually for the worse.

To minimize the risk of damage to the nozzle, bypass the sandpaper and just use the polishing compound. The aggressiveness of the sandpaper

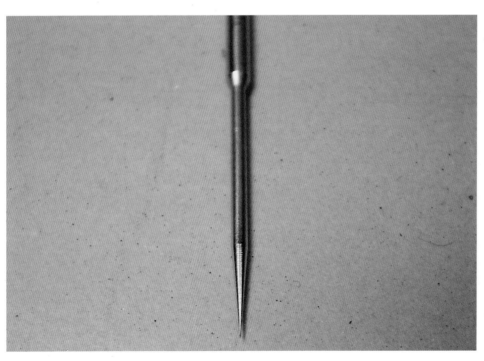

Paasche VL #1 polished needle.

on the delicate edge of the nozzle can quickly cause irreparable damage.

When working with a threaded-type nozzle, we generally remove the needle cap and nozzle cap to expose the nozzle. Then loosen and pull back the needle. It is not necessary to remove the needle, only to withdraw it from the nozzle to protect the tip of the needle. Place a tiny drop of polishing compound on a soft cloth. Pinch the nozzle through the cloth allowing the compound to make contact. Twist your fingers several times until the nozzle has a mirror finish.

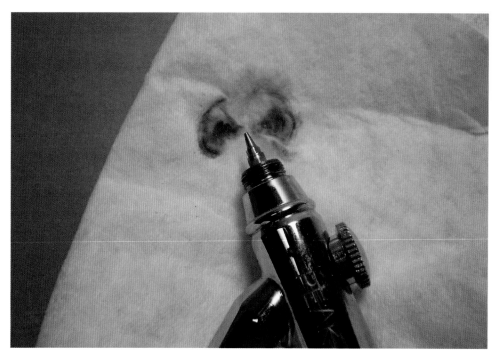

Polishing a screw-in type nozzle.

To polish a self-centered nozzle, remove the nozzle from the airbrush. Place the nozzle firmly on the point of a bamboo meat skewer. Place a small drop of polishing compound on a soft cloth, and pinch the cloth again - making contact with the nozzle and the compound. Twist your fingers several times until the nozzle has a mirror finish.

The combination of these two simple modifications can improve the performance of nearly every airbrush, but again, the greatest improvement will be noticed when they are done to higher detail, smaller nozzle airbrushes.

MODIFYING THE NEEDLE SPRING

As you work with your airbrush you may

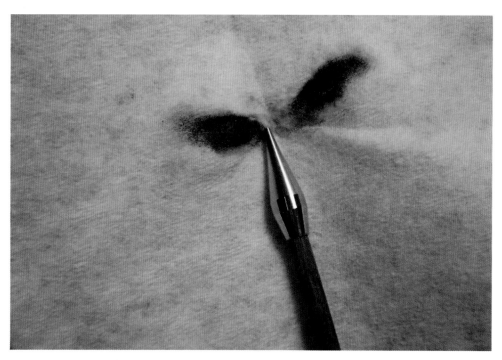

Polishing a self-centering type nozzle.

Factory length needle spring from a Peak X-3.

Needle spring modified to reduce tension on the trigger.

find that the tension on the needle spring or the air valve spring is causing too much resistance, even when it is in its most lax position. It is possible to remove a small section of the springs in the airbrush to relieve tension. A pair of wire cutters will easily cut the soft spring.

You need to address a few concerns before altering the springs in an airbrush. The first is that the ends of the spring are wound in a way such that the ends are parallel to each other. This allows the spring to make complete contact with the body of the airbrush on one end, and the inside of the adjusting sleeve on the other end. Removing the end of the spring may cause it to not make a clean contact inside the brush. The second concern should be obvious; once you remove part of the spring it is impossible to go back and undo it. The only do-over available requires that you first replace the spring with a new one. The best method to ensure that you take off no more than you need is to remove a small piece, then reassemble the brush and try it. If more removal is needed, then repeat the process. This will reduce the risk of removing too much of the spring.

ALTERING THE TRIGGER PAD

The feel and comfort you desire of the trigger pad is completely personal. The pad is the main point of contact with your airbrush and it's important that you are able to work comfortably. Paasche, DeVilbiss, and other manufacturers offer various optional trigger pads for their airbrushes. Generally, these pads simply unscrew from the trigger post and are easily replaced. With other manufacturers that do not offer optional trigger pads, you can do a few things to increase your comfort of use. Some manufacturers may offer rubber add-on pads, such as the Badger series of comfort pads. If these are not available for your airbrush it is possible to shape the very soft chrome-plated brass trigger pad to your own liking with a hand held grinder. Obviously, you must follow all safety rules for the grinder whenever you do this.

Keep in mind again that today's modern airbrushes will usually work extremely well for you right out of the box. The modifications listed in this chapter should only be considered if your particular airbrush does not yield the type of performance your work requires. Also, bear in mind these modifications will only make a good airbrush better, they will not help a poor quality airbrush perform like a higher quality one.

Four optional trigger pads for the DeVilbiss DAGR (left), and the optional rounded Paasche trigger pad.

Badger rubber pad .

Chapter Fourteen

Painting Surfaces

Many to Choose From

The surfaces on which you can use an airbrush are limitless, and new applications are being discovered every day. Any time a liquid needs to be applied to a surface you may find another use for an airbrush. This chapter will look at some of the more common substrates that are used in airbrushing, some of the prep work that needs to be done, as well as noting some of the advantages and disadvantages of each.

PAPER

Paper is one of the most readily available and inexpensive materials to paint on with an airbrush. This surface makes an excellent practice surface and can challenge the artist in many ways. For instance,

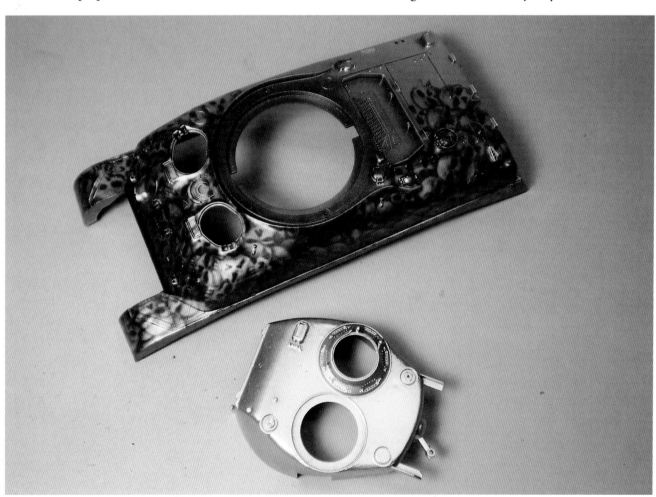

Scale model tank with custom paint.

Custom painted glass.

by using a non-absorbent tracing vellum, the air-brush artist will get the feeling of spraying on primed wood or metal. On the other hand, if the artist chooses to spray on newsprint they will find that the very absorbent paper reacts very much like cloth. While paper can be inexpensive, higher quality papers with greater rag content also make an excellent painting surface.

Paper also makes excellent stencil material. Because it usually has some absorption quality, paint tends not to creep underneath it, ensuring crisp hard edges. Bristol board or card stock is a good example of this kind of paper.

One of the disadvantages of paper is that it tends to be fragile and does not last as long as some other substrates. Consider this if longevity is important for your artwork.

WATERCOLOR PAPER

While watercolor paper should technically be included in the paper category, it has some unique

characteristics that set it apart from its less expensive brothers. First, watercolor paper is generally acid free. This simply means that the acids normally present in paper have been removed. It is acid that causes paper to turn yellow over time. The absence of this ensures your artwork will stay bright and clean.

Watercolor paper also has a higher rag content than other papers. Rag content represents the fibers that make up the paper. The higher the rag content, the stronger the paper. Watercolor paper is also designed to accept a large amount of moisture during the painting process. With this characteristic, spider webbing happens much less frequently.

Watercolor paper is available in different thicknesses that are referred to in pounds. The higher the weight, the thicker the paper. The average is 150 to 300 pounds. In addition, the surface of watercolor paper can range from very smooth to very rough. Smooth surfaces are known as "hot press" and rough surfaces are called "cold press."

ILLUSTRATION BOARD

This very traditional airbrushing substrate has been used for many years. Generally, illustration board is a very high quality, drawing paper permanently mounted on a piece of cardboard. Many of the same variations in watercolor paper apply to illustration board as well. The surfaces are available in both hot and cold press, and most illustration board is also acid free. Because illustration board is rigid, it has an excellent surface for use with frisket and other masking materials that are cut directly on the surface.

T-Shirt design by Scott MacKay.

Different types of paper.

Watercolor paper.

Illustration board.

Nearly any kind of paint can be used on watercolor paper or illustration board. Automotive urethanes do tend to bleed into the fiber of the paper, though, so you probably will want to avoid this surface unless you seal the paper with a basecoat first.

CLOTH

Airbrushing on cloth can range from T-shirts to theater backdrops. Cloth has the ability to absorb a lot of fluid making it very easy to work with. On cloth, the paint does not spider web because it quickly gets absorbed. Most textile makers identify their fabrics according to their composition. If the label says "50/50," the fabric has a makeup of 50 percent cotton and 50 percent synthetic material. Other fabrics may be 100 percent cotton. Each has its advantages and disadvantages.

The 100% cotton cloth has a good heavy feel. The full natural makeup of the material translates to a great ability to absorb paint. On the other hand, paint stands on top of the less absorbent 50/50 material, allowing the finished job to look a bit more vibrant. 50/50 fabric also is lighter weight overall.

Denim is another popular surface for painting. Its pronounced texture makes it catch overspray. With any "fuzzy" material such as denim it is important to lock those fibers down if sharp edges and details are desired. Most manufacturers of fabric paint, such as Createx and Aqua-Flo, offer a clear version of their paint. It is essentially the same paint without any pigment added. When this clear spray is applied to the surface and then heat set it locks all the fibers down and gives an excellent surface to spray on. For practicing, a large sheet, or even paper towels, make excellent and inexpensive material on which to work.

METAL

Painting on a non-absorbent material presents its own set of steps. Preparation is paramount. Most types of paint, especially non-chemically binding paints such as water based paints will not properly adhere unless the correct prep work is done in advance. Despite these additional steps, airbrushing on hard surfaces such as automobiles, motorcycles and signs has become universally popular. Airbrushing on these surfaces works out extremely well given the overall mechanics of the paint. With a car or motorcycle, for example, arriving at the final outcome of a perfectly smooth finish is extremely important. If large amounts of artwork are completed using traditional brushes, edges and ridges can occur as the paint is applied layer after layer. This buildup requires extra work in the end to smooth out with the clear coat. An airbrush, however, applies paint in such thin, controlled layers that it is practically smooth as soon as it is applied. Also, the airbrush applies paint in extremely fine droplets, which gives the clearcoat an excellent surface to adhere to. For practicing, aluminum sign blanks are available from any sign supply house. Most vendors of airbrushes and airbrush supplies also sell blank aluminum license plates that make an excellent inexpensive practice material.

PLASTIC

Scale modeling is vastly popular. The general consensus is that if someone has gone to the trouble of creating an accurate scaled model, then a scaled paint job is by far the best way to finish it. An airbrush atomizes paint just like a spray gun, but on a smaller scale. The same advantages that are gained by using an airbrush on a full size automotive surface apply to scale modeling as well. Everything from perfectly smooth applications of color, to extremely accurate weathering techniques can be achieved. Thinned enamel paints, and water based acrylic, are the kinds of paint most commonly used in scale modeling. With the recent availability of genuine automotive paint in small quantities, however, automotive paint has been gaining in popularity.

FINGERNAILS

The preparation of fingernails is actually very similar to that used for other hard surfaces - including automotive applications. A basecoat is applied first, then the airbrushed artwork, followed by a clear topcoat. This basecoat adheres very well to the fingernail and gives the artwork something solid to stick to. The traditional enamel clearcoat is extremely durable and will keep the artwork safe.

SKIN

Painting on skin, applying body art or temporary tattoos, requires that the skin first be clean and free from oils. This is simply done with a cotton pad and a bit of rubbing alcohol. Care must always be taken on skin, especially around the eyes, nose and mouth. Another very important note is that non-FDA-approved paint should never be used on skin. The airbrush, even on low pressure, is very efficient at

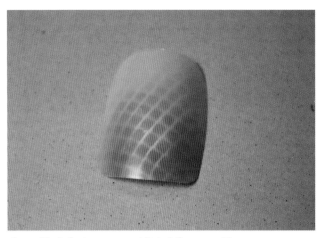

Stenciled design on artificial fingernail.

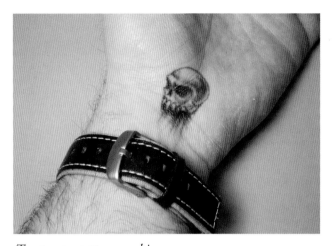

Temporary tattoo on skin.

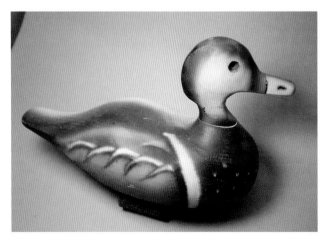

Airbrushing on carved duck decoy.

103

applying paint to the surface of the skin and a hazardous paint has an extremely good chance of entering the body through the subject's pores. Also, use of alcohol based makeup around the face is not recommended - as the airborne alcohol can easily irritate the eyes, nose and mouth.

The use of precut stencils now makes temporary tattoos very easy and yields impressive results, even to those without artistic talent or training. The spray on tanning market has found the use of the airbrush invaluable as well.

WOOD

Woodcarvers have found great uses for the airbrush in their work. Intricately carved pieces are often difficult to paint smoothly with a traditional paint brush. An airbrush allows the artist to get into

Food color airbrushed on a cookie.

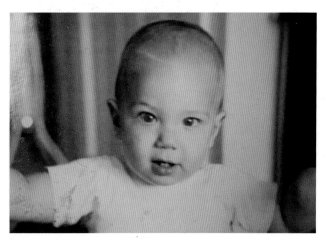

Eyes tinted blue on a black and white photograph.

all the creases and crevasses efficiently. Prep work is generally at a minimum. If a very even coat of transparent color is required, then a sanding sealer is used. If the object is simply going to be painted to look realistic, such as in a duck decoy, often the paint can be applied directly to the unfinished wood. All wood has a degree of absorbency to it, which makes it receptive to nearly all kinds of paint. Smith Paint Company, and other paint manufacturers create specific colors intended for use by wildlife artists. This makes it possible to purchase the exact color you need - without mixing.

TAXIDERMY

Taxidermists and wildlife woodcarvers find themselves looking for the same painting solutions with the airbrush. In some cases, there is just no way to more efficiently apply paint to a complex three dimensional surface. Many industry specific paints are used for taxidermy, yet with a bit of color theory just about any paint system will work.

CERAMIC

Ceramicists rely on the airbrush for everything from even glazes to fine detail. Just as with other hard surfaces, it is often undesirable to have a great amount of paint buildup on the surface. The airbrush is perfectly suited for this application. Smooth transitions of color are possible without ever touching the surface.

The use of the airbrush in ceramics goes beyond creative artwork, though. Bathtub refinishers find the airbrush's ability to flawlessly blend material invaluable when doing touchups and repairs. This job would be nearly impossible with a traditional paint brush.

GLASS

Sign painting on windows and mirrors is very popular. The problem with working on windows is twofold. First the surface is obviously non-porous, making it difficult for most paints to adhere. Second, if working on the outside of a window the paint will be exposed to the weather. If the design is to be long lasting or even permanent, the choice of paint will be crucial. Sign painters' enamel paints are often the best choice for external use. They adhere to any clean surface, do not require a clearcoat and are extremely durable.

Alternatives to the solvent aggressive enamels do exist, however. By painting in reverse with a water-based paint on the inside of the window, the design will remain in place until it is taken down. If the design is seasonal, then look for commercially available, water based window paint. Water-based automotive paint also works extremely well for temporary designs.

FOOD

Food coloring can be applied easily to any food surface. Cakes and cookies can have anything from a basic color change to incredibly detailed artwork. Without question, nothing should be put on a food product that is not recommended for consumption. Food coloring is by far the most popular choice - given its strength in color, thin viscosity and ease of spraying. Many other consumables that can be sprayed only require you to look at the viscosity to aid you in choosing the correct airbrush for the job.

It is strongly recommended that if you intend to airbrush consumables that you keep a dedicated airbrush for that job alone. The risk of residual paint and solvents being left behind in an airbrush, and that these will eventually end up on the food that you are spraying, is much too high.

PHOTOGRAPHS

Prior to the 1950s the major use of airbrushes was in retouching and coloring photographs. While the process today is easily done to digital photos with computer software, an art form in altering existing photographic prints is still present. Color keying black and white photographs to a specific page in a scrapbook, adding special effect fades and blacking out unwanted sections of the images are all possible with an airbrush. Depending on the surface on which the photograph is printed, the choice of paints used generally follows the same path as for use with paper. Water based acrylics, inks and dyes make excellent choices.

WALLS

Mural work on interior and exterior walls has become a high art. Just as in other forms of fine art, multiple techniques are drawn together to create fantastic works of art. Paint choices for these projects share some of the same concerns as the window paintings. Working indoors and out of the direct sunlight will allow you to use a paint that is much different from a paint that is designed to withstand the weather and direct sunlight.

Once the correct paint is chosen, you can approach the project in many ways. One of the most common ways is to block large areas of the work in with traditional brushes and rollers, leaving all the fading and blending for the airbrush and spray guns. Regardless of how you proceed, look carefully at the job you need the spray equipment to do and choose it for those requirements. Match it up to the paint and it will perform flawlessly for you.

IN SUMMARY

This very small list of substrates barely scratches the surface of what can be sprayed on, and the projects you and your airbrush will be able to complete. Constantly search "outside the box" for new applications and your discoveries will profoundly impact your current abilities. We all learn by the challenges we face. By working with different applications your skill will grow quickly.

Wall mural.

Chapter Fifteen

Chapter Painting Basics

Proper Performance and Mastery of The Basics

Understanding how an airbrush works plays a major role in keeping things operating properly. Equally important is a basic understanding of the fundamental control of the airbrush. When you are in control of the airbrush you will encounter far fewer operational problems as you work.

While some artistic tools have countless foundational techniques, the airbrush only has a few, the mastery of which will ensure you great control. This chapter will look at these rudimentary

Holding the airbrush between the middle finger and thumb leaves the index finger free to operate the main lever.

strokes and show you the techniques you need to master them.

The manner in which you hold the airbrush will be determined by your own personal comfort. The standard method of holding the airbrush is to grip the air valve body with your thumb and middle finger. This allows your index finger to rest on the main lever. It is important to continuously check your grip on the airbrush as you perform these exercises. Your attention in the beginning will be focused on performing the actions involved in the exercise, and you my not realize the tension that is developing in your grip. If you notice this heightened grip or start to experience pain, take a break and stretch your hand. As you become more comfortable with these exercises the tension in your grip will ease.

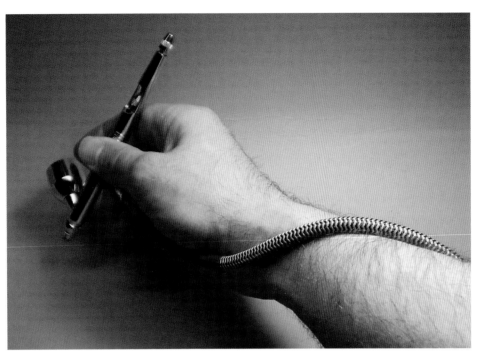

Draping the air hose over the wrist keeps it from dragging through the wet paint.

The air hose attaches to the bottom of the airbrush. It can be simply left to hang below the airbrush or, if necessary, wrapped over the wrist to keep it out of the way.

The first and most important rule of airbrush use is to remember that air is what powers the entire process. In a double-action airbrush you control the introduction of air by depressing the main lever. For all of the following fundamental strokes remembering to keep the air flowing without breaks will ensure that everything operates smoothly.

Painting a page of dots.

The fundamental rule for all these airbrush strokes is - air on, paint on, paint off, air off. If more than one exercise is performed the air is kept on continuously until all the painting is done. The main lever is then released, turning off the air. It is the rush of air across the tip of the nozzle that creates the vacuum which pulls the paint through the airbrush. Stopping the airflow prematurely causes the paint to draw back into the airbrush and causes a delay in spraying the following strokes. The rush of air is also what atomizes the paint off of the needle. Keeping the air flowing atomizes all of the paint from the needle. If the air is turned off when paint is still on the needle it can cause the paint to dry and clog the airbrush, stopping it from working. This is commonly called tip dry. Tip dry can easily be removed by carefully picking off the paint with your finger nails or brushed off with a paint brush dipped in cleaner. Regardless of the paint, tip dry will occur. Removing it frequently keeps the airbrush operating.

Learning three fundamental strokes, and one additional stroke, will help you get the most out of your airbrush. The first is the Dot stroke. In this stroke the goal is to create a simple dot. To begin this stroke, load the airbrush with paint, aim it at the surface - with the airbrush about six to eight inches away from a sheet of practice paper and press the main lever to begin the flow of air.

The next step is to very gradually begin pulling the main lever back. The goal here may seem to be to make a small dot of paint. However, that is secondary to the real goal, which is to get a feel for how the paint atomizes out of the airbrush. As you very slowly draw the main lever back, the paint will gradually appear on the surface you are painting. Don't let the paint come out too fast. Again, the goal is to make the dot appear very slowly - like an old Polaroid photograph. Paint several of these slow developing dots without stopping the flow of air between doing them.

Once you get comfortable with the action involved in creating the dots at that distance, try moving the airbrush closer to the surface. You will notice that the main lever does not need to be pulled back as far to get a dark dot as it did at the earlier, greater distance. This technique will take more control to keep the paint from spider webbing. That is what you get when the wet paint on the surface is pushed in all directions by the rush of air, leaving thin fingers of paint radiating from the dot.

As you begin to master the dot at close range you will also notice the dots are very sharp and tight, unlike the softer, more diffused dot created when the airbrush is held farther from the surface. Your distance from the surface will play a major role in the different

Painting the line stroke.

effects you will be able to create with the airbrush. Work with a variety of distances until you are comfortable.

The next fundamental airbrush stroke is the line. The line stroke builds on the techniques learned while perfecting the dot. With the line stroke, keep the airbrush about four inches from the surface and begin the flow of air. Then begin the flow of paint as you did to create the dot. Once the paint is flowing, move your hand across the surface creating a line. When you reach the end of the line, while holding the main lever down, smoothly push it forward to stop the flow of paint. It is very important here to keep the air-flow going, even though you have ended the paint flow. This will clean off any paint that is left on the tip of the needle. Otherwise, when you turn on the air to create the next line, the residual paint will spit out onto your surface.

Just as you did with the dot, create as many lines as you can to get a true feel for how the air-brush works. You should notice some things as you work on this exercise. First is that all the characteristics of the airbrush you discovered while practicing the dot apply to the line stroke as well. The farther you are from the surface, the softer and more diffused your line will be; the closer to the surface you are, the crisper and more defined your work will look.

During the beginning stages of learning the line stroke, your practice may appear wavy and uneven. Smooth and straight lines come from two things. The first is speed of movement. If you move your hand quickly across the surface while creating your line you will notice that it gets smoother almost immediately. Second is that larger mus-

cle groups in your arms produce a smoother line than the smaller muscle groups in your hands. This means that if you are standing during this exercise and you rotate your torso to move the air-brush across the surface, the line will be smoother than if you simply moved your hand to create the line. In addition to that, many artists steady their airbrushing hand with their other hand. By cup-ping the heel of your airbrushing hand in your other hand you will add stability to your strokes. This technique can be applied to anything you do with the airbrush.

The muscles in your hands and arms feel most comfortable working in a certain direction. This is called Range of Motion. As you work you will find that moving in one direction will be far more comfortable than the other. Practice this line stroke in many different directions. By doing this you will expand your range of motion and your airbrush strokes will be much smoother.

As you get the creation of smooth straight lines down, move on to lines that are wavy and have different directions. This will challenge your range of motion even further, and increase your

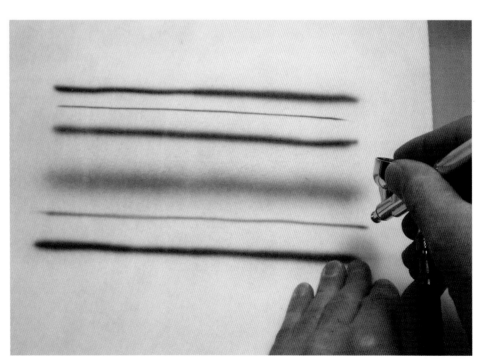

Lines painted at different distances from the surface.

Wavy lines based on the standard line stroke.

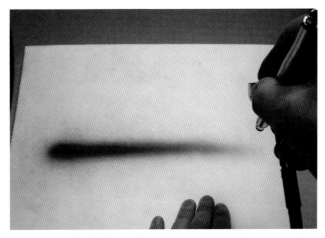

Creating the fade stroke.

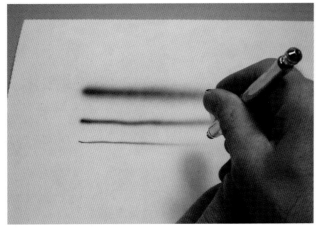

Fade strokes painted at different distances from the surface.

skill with the airbrush. Throughout all these exercises be mindful of the paint that is building up on the tip of the airbrush, and also of the strength of your grip. Tip dry not cleaned off the airbrush will quickly block the nozzle cap and stop the flow of paint. Excessive tension in your grip on the airbrush will quickly cause fatigue.

The third of the basic strokes is the fade stroke. Like the line stroke, the fade builds on the skills that you have gained by practicing the previous strokes. To begin, hold the airbrush about eight inches from the surface and press the trigger to start the flow of air. Next, draw the lever back to introduce the paint. When the paint is flowing, move your airbrush hand across the surface. From there, very slowly push the main lever forward to decrease the flow of paint until it is completely off - as you continue to move across the surface. Continue the airflow without paint to end the stroke. What you should have when you are finished is a line stroke that slowly fades away to nothing.

The same range of motion exercises previously described should be applied to the fade stroke. On some occasions turning the surface that you are working on won't be possible. Being able to perform the fade stroke in different directions will be extremely valuable.

The fade stroke is easily one of the most important rudimentary strokes of all. Mastery of this stroke allows you to blend colors on the surface, create seamless washes, and do perfect shading. Of all the control strokes, this one is used the most.

As you practice the fade, look back at all the strokes with which you have covered your page. Undoubtedly a few will look as though they end in a sharp point rather than a smooth fade. In these instances you were moving closer to the surface at the same time you were slowly stopping the paint flow. This is actually called a dagger or rat tail stroke.

Again, the techniques for creating the dagger stroke are exactly the same as the fade stroke with the exception of the airbrush moving closer to the surface as the stroke is being ended. Normally, the

110

dagger stroke will occur naturally as you practice the fade stroke. The key to successfully creating the dagger stroke is to have complete control over the fade stroke. Then, by simply moving your hand closer to the surface you will have created the dagger stroke. This is a difficult stroke to learn as it stands by itself, but by mastering the fade stroke first, the dagger stroke will more natural and easy.

The dagger stroke demonstrates the true potential of the airbrush. In one stroke you will have created a full range of effects from a soft fuzzy line to an extremely sharp pinpoint line. This is also the airbrush stroke that is used to create extremely fine details. The soft beginning of this stroke primes the paint through the airbrush and keeps the paint flowing smoothly for the minute details. As with the other strokes, practicing the dagger in many different directions will expand your range of movement and make all aspects of airbrushing easier.

Practicing these basic strokes can take many forms. Some people respond to a regimented practice schedule. For example, each day before working on any projects, they will fill a complete page with each stroke. Each is drawn while carefully and slowly making sure all aspects of the techniques are followed. Others prefer a looser approach, perhaps simply applying the techniques while they work. Use whichever method works best for you, but take learning these fundamentals very seriously. Becoming completely familiar with them so they are second nature will profoundly affect your performance and that of your airbrush.

The analogy of the professional athlete applies here. Having the most technologically advanced golf club won't necessarily make you a better golfer, but if someone has mastered the fundamentals of the game of golf they will benefit from the edge that a state-of-the-art club can give. Practice seriously with your airbrushing, but find a way to make it enjoyable at the same time and the rewards will be enormous.

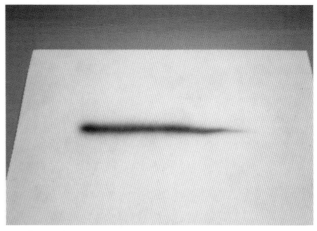

Fade stroke that sharpens at the end rather than simply fading away.

Painting a dagger stroke.

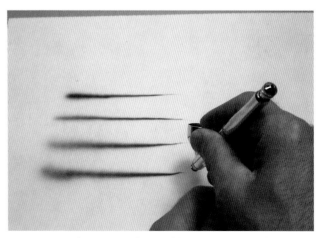

Dagger strokes painted at different distances from the surface.

Chapter Sixteen

Airbrush Buyers' Guide

A Comprehensive Comparison

With so many different brands and styles of airbrushes on the market, the choices can be overwhelming. Knowing the answers to some basic questions can help you narrow your selection, and direct you to the exact airbrush you need.

In addition, by understanding how airbrushes work you will see that, despite their superficial differences, most airbrushes operate the same way. Their variations are in specific adjustments that allow them to perform certain roles better than others.

Ask yourself some of these key questions to real-

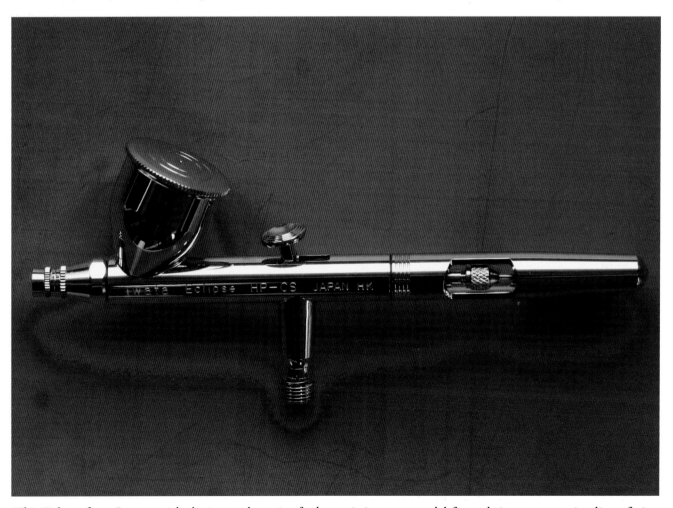

This Eclipse from Iwata, with the integral gravity-feed cup, is just one model from their very extensive line of airbrushes. Be sure to buy an airbrush that matches your needs.

ly narrow down your search for that brand new airbrush. Armed with these answers when you begin your search, you will have a much better idea of the tool that will serve your needs.

Your first consideration is going to be your budget. How much do you have to spend on the initial purchase, and what are you willing to invest in such wear and tear parts as the tips and needles? Some airbrushes are like exotic cars and have proportionately high maintenance costs. Knowing your budget going in allows you to comfortably operate your airbrushes without excessive expenditures.

The second question to ask yourself is, "What type of airbrushing are you planning to do?" An airbrush that is suited for painting T-shirts would be extremely hard to handle if used to paint designs on fingernails.

Knowing what kind of work you hope to do goes hand in hand with knowing what kind of paint you intend to use. Some airbrushes can process thicker paint than others. Some airbrushes are better suited for solvent based paints. Being aware of the type of paint you plan to use will ensure that the airbrush you choose will not let you down.

How often you intend to use your airbrush is also important. If you see yourself spraying commercially, and very often - for long periods of time you should consider buying several brushes to ensure that your work is not interrupted by downtime. On the other hand, hobbyists who will only be spraying occasionally may find they have plenty of time to maintain their airbrush as they need it.

Your workspace may also be affected by the amount of time you decide to spend painting. A full production airbrush shop requires a vastly different space than the person who picks up the airbrush once in a while for personal enjoyment.

Again, knowing the answers to these questions

A miniature moisture trap may include a small drain valve; it will act as the last barrier for moisture in the air lines.

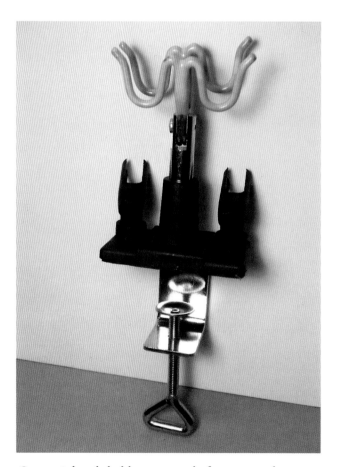

Some airbrush holders are made for two, and some will handle as many as eight brushes. The correct one will keep your idle airbrushes safe from damage.

A miniature pressure valve may be used to separately preset the airflow into the airbrush, independent of the adjustments available on the brush.

can go a long way in helping you avoid surprises as you get set up.

The airbrush chart included with this chapter is different from most of the other cross-reference charts you may see. The information given here allows you to match the answers from the core questions above to the airbrush that may best suit your needs. It is important to remember that the chart offers only a guideline. Your personal preferences in the end will determine the brush that will work right for you. Your qualifications might lead you to an airbrush you normally would not have chosen. Remember, your comfort with the tool, matched with that tool's ability to perform properly will produce some amazing results.

Matching the compressor with the airbrush is also important. Being aware of issues such as how the people around you will be affected by the noise your airbrush compressor makes will help you choose the right setup for your workspace.

A number of accessories should be considered when selecting your airbrush. The first is a good, solid airbrush holder. Some models hold two and some will handle as many as eight. Determine how many airbrushes you will need to have set up and then get a holder to accommodate all of them. This will keep your idle airbrushes out of the way and safe from damage by being knocked to the floor.

A miniature moisture trap can be attached directly to the airbrush or clamped into

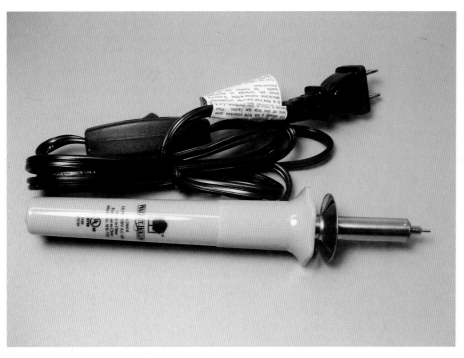

If you can't find what you need ready-made, you can use a hand held stencil burner to cut your own out of many different stencil materials.

the air hose. It will act as the last barrier for moisture in the air lines. These traps may include a small drain valve.

Small air pressure valves are also available for your airbrush. These devices are used to directly adjust the airflow into the airbrush.

Precut stencils can save you time in laying out repetitive patterns. Several manufacturers provide numerous different shapes to accommodate any design need. If you can't find exactly the right template, stencil burners make quick work of cutting your own. These hand held burners heat up and their sharp tips easily burn through many different kinds of stencil material.

AIRBRUSHES COMPARED

The following charts are designed to give you an overview of how some of the most popular airbrushes on the market compare with one another. We have chosen not to focus on specific jobs for which these different airbrushes could be used. Rather, this information is compiled to give you a very basic, practical starting point to begin narrowing the possible choices of airbrushes down to those most capable of filling your needs.

Model - indicates the name of the airbrush in the manufacturer's line
Trigger Type - designates whether the airbrush has a double, single or fixed - action trigger.
Paint Feed - designates the style of paint feed for the airbrush: gravity, siphon or side-fed
Tip Size - indicates the measurement of the opening across the tip of the nozzle.
Paint Viscosity - indicates the thickness of the paint that is intended to be used in the airbrush, e.g., light (inks and dyes), medium (acrylics and automotive basecoats), heavy (Latex and craft paint).
Spray Pattern - indicates the quality of the recommended paint's atomization - fine, medium or coarse.
Cost - Low, less than $75; Moderate, between $75 and $175; High, more than $175
Use - Some airbrushes are designed for specific uses, as noted, others can be used for so many things they are difficult, if not impossible, to categorize.

Notes:
(1) Interchangeable tips and needles allow for various multiple set ups.
(2) AB Turbine is unique and does not use a traditional nozzle.

Model Trigger	Type	Paint Feed	Nozzle size	Paint viscosity	Atomization	Cost	Use
Aztec							
430	Double	Side	(1)	Medium	Medium	Moderate	Versatility
470	Double	Side	(1)	Medium	Medium	Moderate	Versatility
480	Double	Side	(1)	Medium	Medium	Moderate	Versatility
220	Single	Side	(1)	Medium	Medium	Low	Versatility
270	Single	Side	(1)	Medium	Medium	Low	Versatility
320	Single	Side	(1)	Medium	Medium	Low	Versatility
Badger							
Sotar 20/20	Double	Gravity	.19mm	Light	Fine	High	Detail
155 Anthem	Double	Siphon	.76mm	Medium	Medium	Moderate	Versatility
360 Universal	Double	Siphon/Gravity	.76mm	Medium	Medium	Moderate	Versatility
175 Crescendo	Double	Siphon	(1)	Medium	Medium	Moderate	Versatility
100SF	Double	Side	.51mm	Light	Fine	Moderate	Detail
100LG	Double	Gravity	.51mm	Medium	Medium	Moderate	Detail
100G	Double	Gravity	.51mm	Light	Fine	Moderate	Detail
100SG	Double	Gravity	.51mm	Light	Fine	Moderate	Detail
150	Double	Siphon	(1)	Medium	Medium	Moderate	Versatility
Renegade Velocity	Double	Gravity	.21mm	Light	Fine	Moderate	Detail
Renegade Rage	Double	Siphon	.21mm	Light	Fine	Moderate	Detail
Renegade Spirit	Double	Side	.21mm	Light	Fine	Moderate	Detail
Colani							
Colani	Double	Gravity	.4mm	Light/Med	Fine	High	

Model Trigger	Type	Paint Feed	Nozzle size	Paint viscosity	Atomization	Cost	Use
DeVilbiss							
DAGR	Double	Gravity	.35mm	Light/Med	Med	Moderate	
EFBE							
Titan	Double	Gravity	.15mm	Light	Fine	High	Detail
A	Double	Gravity	.15mm	Light	Fine	High	
B	Double	Gravity	.3mm	Light	Fine	High	
B1	Double	Side	.3mm	Light	Fine/Med	High	
C1	Double	Side	.3mm	Light	Fine/Med	High	
B2	Double	Side	.4mm	Med	Med	High	
C2	Double	Side	.4mm	Med	Med	High	
Artis 1	Double	Gravity	.3mm	Light	Fine	High	Detail
Artis 2	Double	Side	.3mm	Light/Med	Fine	High	
Graffo							
T1	Double	Gravity	.15mm	Light	Fine	High	
T2	Double	Side	.2mm	Light	Fine	High	Detail
T3	Double	Side	.4mm	Med	Med	High	
Ultra X	Double	Siphon	.4mm	Med	Med	Moderate	
Hansa							
Evolution							
Solo	Double	Gravity	.2mm	Light	Fine	High	Detail
2 in 1	Double	Gravity	.4mm	Med	Med	High	
X	Double	Siphon	.6mm	Heavy	Coarse	High	
Infinity							
Solo	Double	Gravity	.15mm	Light	Fine	High	Detail
Iwata							
CMC Plus	Double	Gravity	.23mm	Light	Fine	High	Extreme Detail
CMC	Double	Gravity	.23mm	Light	Fine	High	Extreme Detail
CMB	Double	Gravity	.18mm	Light	Fine	High	Extreme Detail
CMSB	Double	Side	.18mm	Thin	Light	Fine	Extreme Detail
AH	Double	Gravity	.2mm	Light	Fine	High	Detail
BH	Double	Gravity	.2mm	Light	Fine	High	Detail
CH	Double	Gravity	.3mm	Light/Med	Light	High	
A Plus	Double	Gravity	.2mm	Light	Fine	High	Detail
B Plus	Double	Gravity	.2mm	Light	Fine	High	Detail
C Plus	Double	Gravity	.3mm	Light	Fine /Med	High	
BC Plus	Double	Siphon	.3mm	Light	Fine /Med	High	
SB Plus	Double	Side	.2mm	Light	Fine	High	Detail
SBS	Double	Side	.35mm	Light/Med	Fine	Moderate	Detail
CS	Double	Gravity	.35mm	Light/Med	Fine	Moderate	Detail
BCS	Double	Siphon	.5mm	Med	Medm	Moderate	
BS	Double	Gravity	.35mm	Light/Med	Fine	Moderate	Detail
KCH	Double	Gravity	.3mm	Light	Fine	High	Detail
KCM	Double	Gravity	.23mm	Light	Fine	High	Detail
KCS	Double	Gravity	.35mm	Light/Med	Fine	High	Detail
KTH	Fixed Double	Gravity	. 5mm	Med	Med	High	
KTR	Fixed Double	Gravity	.3mm	Light/Med	Fine	High	
AR	Double	Gravity	.3mm	Light	Fine	Moderate	Detail
BR	Double	Gravity	.3mm	Light	Fine	Moderate	Detail
CR	Double	Gravity	.5mm	Medium	Medium	Moderate	
BCR	Double	Siphon	.5mm	Medium	Medium	Moderate	
SAR	Single	Siphon	.5mm	Medium	Medium	Moderate	
TR-1	Fixed Double	Side	.3mm	Light/Med	Med	Moderate	
TR-2	Fixed Double	Side	.5mm	Med	Med	Moderate	

Model Trigger	Type	Paint Feed	Nozzle size	Paint viscosity	Atomization	Cost	Use
Paasche							
VL	Double	Siphon	(1)	Med	Med/Heavy	Moderate	Versatility
Talon	Double	Gravity	x	Med/Light	Fine	Moderate	Versatility
VSR90	Double	Gravity	.25mm	Light	Fine	Moderate	Detail
Millennium	Double	Siphon	.73mm	Medium	Medium	Moderate	Versatility
H	Single	Siphon	(1)	Medium	Medium	Moderate	Versatility/Coverage
AB Turbine	Double	Gravity	(2)	Light	Fine	High	Detail
V	Double	Siphon	(1)	Light	Fine	Moderate	Detail
Peak							
C5	Double	Gravity	.3mm	Light	Fine	Moderate	Detail
X3	Double	Siphon	.5mm	Medium	Medium	Low	
X5	Double	Siphon	.5mm	Medium	Medium	Moderate	
Precision Aire							
APD	Double	Siphon	.5mm	Medium	Medium	Moderate	
XFS	Double	Gravity	.3mm	Light	Fine	Moderate	Detail
APT	Double	Gravity	.5mm	Medium	Medium	Moderate	
XFS Treo	Double	Gravity	.3mm	Light	Fine	Moderate	Detail
Richpen							
Phoenix 213	Double	Gravity	.3mm	Light	Fine	High	Detail
Spectra 033	Double	Siphon	.3mm	Thin	Light	Moderate	Detail
Spectra 013	Single	Gravity	.3mm	Light	Fine	Moderate	Detail
Apollo 112A	Double	Gravity	.2mm	Light	Fine	Moderate	Detail
Apollo 112B	Double	Gravity	.2mm	Light	Fine	Moderate	Detail
Apollo 113C	Double	Gravity	.3mm	Light	Fine	Moderate	Detail
Mojo	Double	Gravity	.2mm	Light	Fine	High	Extreme Detail
GP-S1	Fixed Double	Side	.2mm	Light	Fine	Moderate	Detail
GP-1	Fixed Double	Side	.3mm	Light	Fine	Moderate	Detail
GP-2	Fixed Double	Side	x	Medium	Medium	Moderate	Fine coverage
ES-6	Fixed Double	Side	x	Medium	Medium	High	Coverage
Silverline							
M	Double	Side	.4mm	Medium	Medium	High	
Limited Edition	Double	Gravity	.2mm	Light	Fine	High	Detail
Tamiya							
Trigger Type	Fixed Double	Gravity	.2mm	Light	Fine	Moderate	
HG Superfine	Double	Gravity	.2mm	Fine	Fine	Moderate	
HG2	Double	Gravity	.3mm	Fine	Fine	Moderate	
Workwide	Fixed Double	Gravity	.5mm	Medium	Medium	Moderate	
Topline							
181	Double	Gravity	.2mm	Light	Fine	Moderate	Detail
281	Double	Gravity	.2mm	Light	Fine	Moderate	Detail
381	Double	Gravity	.3mm	Light/Medium	Medium	Moderate	Hobby
481	Double	Side	.3mm	Light/Medium	Medium	Moderate	
581	Double	Gravity	.2mm	Light	Fine	Moderate	
681	Double	Siphon	.3mm	Light/Medium	Medium	Moderate	
Vega							
1000	Double	Gravity	.5	Medium	Medium	Moderate	
2000	Double	Siphon	(1)	Medium	Medium	Moderate	
3000	Double	Siphon	.5	Medium	Medium	Moderate	
4000	Double	Gravity	.5	Medium	Medium	Moderate	
5000	Double	Gravity	.5	Medium	Medium	Moderate	
6000	Double	Side	.5	Medium	Medium	Moderate	

Chapter Seventeen

Stencils, Templates and Masks

Creating Effects

While it is possible to refine your freehand skills to a degree that will allow you to create some very sharp and controlled edges with your airbrush - templates, stencils and masks can make some jobs go much more quickly. Amazing textures can be created with their assistance in a fraction of the time than it would take to paint without them. In this chapter, we will look at how these tools can enhance what the airbrush is capable of doing on its own. Just as knowing how the airbrush operates makes everything easier, knowing the different characteristics of the masking materials you will be

Many airbrush shields, templates and stencils are available.

using will make the painting process go much more smoothly. The challenge comes in understanding what each of the masking materials can offer you and when is the best time to use each one.

Here are a few simple projects that will give you a feel for each one and help you determine which one will be best.

Precut, loose templates come in an incredible variety of shapes and sizes. Their curves and edges are designed to match every conceivable shape. The advantage of these templates is that they arc very quick to use, allowing you to be spontaneous in your work while still giving you the ability to create sharp, hard edges. Knowing the limitations of your airbrush will help you determine which of the hand held shields will help you reach the desired results.

One thing that most commercially cut templates have in common is that a large number of shapes are often packed into each template. It takes a bit of practice to limit your use to just the area of the template that you would like. As you begin to work with them you will notice if you spray the area you want from a distance, you will also get faint overspray on your work in areas of the template you weren't intending to use. Here is a great exercise that will help you gain control in working with these templates.

Begin by cutting a circle out of a piece of card stock or plastic. Make sure the circle is large enough that it comes close to the outer edge of the stencil material. For example, when using a 5x5-inch square of card stock, cut a four-inch circle from the middle of it. This will place the edge of the circle about a half inch from the four outer edges of the square. Next, cut the card stock in half so you are left with two half circles.

The goal for this exercise is to paint a complete, smooth circle, without any overspray at the edges of the template.

Keeping in mind how the airbrush delivers paint will help you master the techniques needed to create this circle. The first thing to consider is the template itself. Look at it and you will see which areas might give you some trouble. These would be in the areas of the template that you intend to use that are very close to other elements on the template that you do not intend to use. In our exercise,

Using a roll of tape to draw the circle (Inset) Completed circle exercise template.

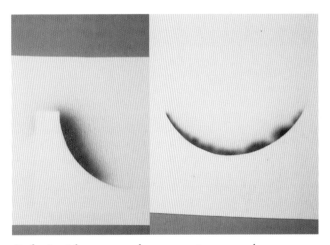

Left: Avoid overspray by not getting near the corners. Right: If you are too close to the template the spray will not be smooth.

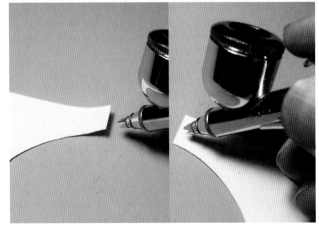

Left: Aiming at the edge of the template will push it up. Right: Spraying with the template holds it down.

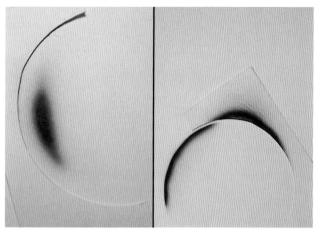

Left: Use the fade stroke on this exercise.
Right: Rotate the template to complete the circle.

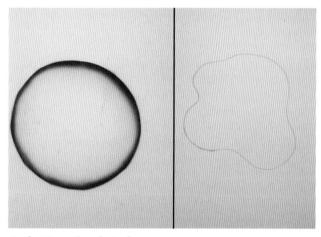

Left: Completed circle
Right: Drawing a random blob shape

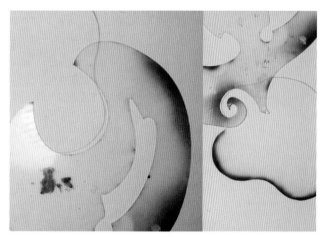

Left: Match stencil to curve on drawing.
Right: Continue matching curves as you paint the outline.

this would be where the circle pattern comes closest to the outer edge of the card. It would be very easy to overspray these areas and see the unwanted halo of that shape in your work. Areas of the template, such as the corners of the square, give more protection from this overspray.

The second thing to consider is the distance you hold the airbrush from the work surface while painting. Holding the brush too far away will cause overspray - though the blends will be smooth; hold it too close and the chance of overspray is reduced, but it is more difficult to get a smooth blend. The template you use will determine how far from the surface you will be able to work. As you get more comfortable with the templates you will develop a natural feel for this balance.

One last factor to consider as you get ready to do this exercise is what the force of the air from the airbrush will do to the template while spraying. If you spray against the edge of the template *(see photos)*, the air will lift the template off the surface and paint will get underneath, this is called underspray. By spraying with the edge of the template, the edge will be held down by the air and a very sharp edge will result.

With these things in mind you can begin to create your circle. The stroke to use here is a fade stroke that will allow the next section of the circle to be blended seamlessly into this one. This template has an outside length of five inches, so with this gravity fed airbrush I am keeping about one inch from the surface while I am spraying. Again, with a bigger template that has more coverage, the airbrush could be moved farther away to give smoother blends, but that is not the purpose of this exercise. Experiment with different distances to get a feel for what will give you the best results.

Once this section of the circle is painted in, rotate the template so that the same part of the template will be in position for the next section. When finished with this section continue to rotate the template until the entire circle is completed. Remember the airbrushing basics while you work. Keep the air on all the time and work in light, controlled layers. When finished, you should have a continuous circle with no overspray at the edges.

Keep in mind, this is an exercise to challenge

you and develop your skills, it is not the most efficient way to mask and paint a circle. If the goal were simply to create a circle, it would be quicker to cut the same size circle out of a larger piece of card stock. With that template it would be much easier to produce a clean, tight circle.

Once you have gotten a feel for the things that you need to think about, and do, to control under- and overspray you can move on to the next exercise. For this you can use a precut template, or you can cut your own template again from cardstock or plastic. The template should have many curves of different sizes and lengths. Next, on your work surface, lightly draw a random blob shape. The goal here will be to fill the inside of this shape, using the template of curves that you cut out earlier.

Find the curve on your template that most closely matches the curve in your drawing. Keep in mind the techniques you have learned in the circle exercise and begin spraying. Find the next curve and continue around the entire edge until the shape is finished. Again, the goal is the same as the circle exercise - smooth fill, sharp edges without any overspray.

Image templates have become extremely popular as well. Nearly every image that you can imagine can be found in a precut stencil. The idea behind these templates is that they give the artist the ability to lay down the foundation of the image very quickly and simply. Using these types of templates require the same techniques that are involved with the use of generic shaped patterns. Managing underspray, overspray, and keeping an eye on adjacent shapes will help to ensure these tools give you everything they are designed to do.

There are two types of image templates. The first produces a positive image, which means that the areas you are spraying are actually the object itself. The second kind of image template is a negative template. This defines the shape of the image by allowing you to spray the background. The color of the surface you are working on, and the style of the image that you are trying to achieve, will determine whether you need a positive or negative template. The following sequences describe the creation of an image using a positive template.

Positive image template

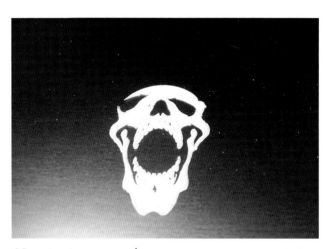

Negative image template

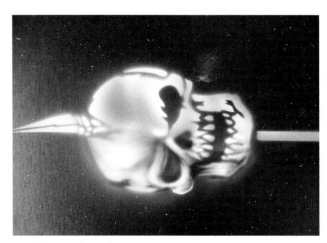

Add green for color.

121

Clouds created with torn paper.

Clouds created with torn scuff pad.

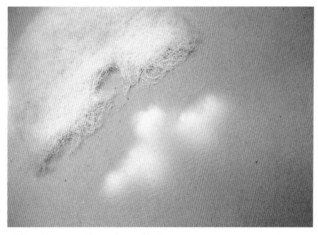

Clouds created with pulled cotton.

The first thing to do is to cover up the unwanted images on the template so they don't produce ghosted overspray on your surface. The skull chosen could be sprayed while the others remained uncovered, but the additional time spent avoiding overspray could be better spent working on the desired image.

A very light mist across the whole area will set up the image. From there shading and shadow can be applied using the shapes of the template to keep the edges sharp and clean. By using different parts of the template it is easy to add various elements to the existing image.

WORKING WITH TEXTURES

An airbrush gives the user great control. Paint can be sprayed onto a surface through many different materials to create complex patterns such as lace and diamonds that would take an extremely long time to paint traditionally.

Clouds can be quickly rendered using torn paper, stretched cotton or pieces of torn scuff pads. By spraying paint along these different types of edges, very realistic clouds can be created. When spraying through a piece of material such as this, it helps to remain very close to the surface to keep the paint concentrated. That will help to show off the texture. The airbrush should be perpendicular to the surface when spraying through this type of material. Having the airbrush perpendicular helps to hold the material down and concentrates the spray evenly through the mask.

The photos show the different effects that can be used to get the look of clouds. The first example uses a simple piece of torn paper. Treat the paper as you would any hand held template. Spray with the edge to hold the paper down. Work in light layers and build up the color slowly. Using different sections of the edge, and flipping the paper over, will keep the work looking completely random.

The second cloud sequence uses a torn scuff pad. The edge of the pad is similar to the torn paper, but because of the loose fibers that make up the pad some paint is allowed to pass through, giving a different effect. Here again it works well if the airbrush is held perpendicular to the scuff pad and remains close to the work. The concentrated spray drives itself through the pad and gives a very distinct look.

Finally, by gently pulling apart a cotton ball and using the edge, an even softer cloud shape can be achieved. Soft, difficult-to-control templates such as a cotton ball are easily blown around by the air from the airbrush. It helps to hold the cotton ball between two fingers and spray the section of the cotton in between.

Complex textures can be created more easily by using such things as lace and fishnet material. Simply stretching the material over the surface and spraying through it will create a negative image of the pattern in the material.

Check the photos to see how to create a snake-skin pattern using fishnet material. On the black background, stretch the fishnet material over the surface. Starting with white, a diamond-shaped pattern is sprayed through the material. Keeping the airbrush four to five inches from the surface will keep the diamond pattern fairly soft and loose. Once the overall pattern is painted with the white, the color is introduced. Working from light to dark choose yellow first. With the airbrush six to seven inches away, spray the larger areas with the yellow. The next color to be used is red, and it is applied from the same distance as the yellow was. Black is next to lightly shade the lower right side of each diamond. When applying the shading the airbrush should be the same distance from the surface as it was when spraying the red and yellow. Take care to apply this shading in very light layers and to clean any tip dry off frequently to avoid any paint blow outs. Last is the application of the highlights using white in a long straight line. Exactly the same technique is used here as in the shading. Stay at the same distance from the surface, work slowly and control the tip dry. The results can be very realistic with minimal effort.

Another kind of masking material commonly used to enhance the performance of an airbrush is the adhesive mask. Adhesive masks have the advantage of staying put during use, giving an extremely sharp edge. They can often be cut in very detailed and intricate ways. This type of masking can be done with material that can be cut and temporarily attached to your work surface. Some common adhesive masks include standard masking tape, automotive fine line tape, vinyl paint mask and frisket.

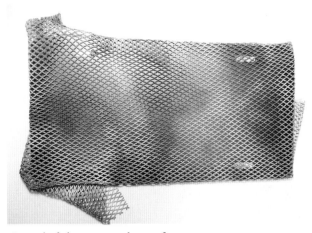

Stretch fishnet over the surface.

Create diamond shapes with white paint.

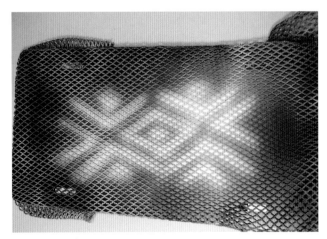

Lightly mist yellow over the entire surface.

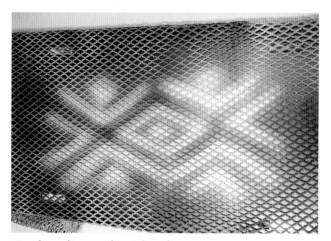

Outline diamonds with red.

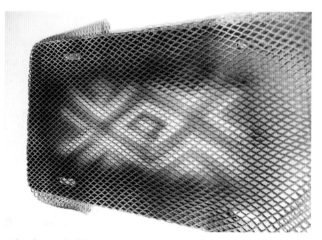

Shade with black.

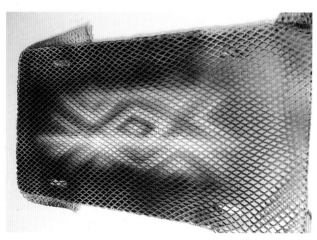

Add white highlights.

You may also create your own adhesive masks. Commercially available repositionable adhesive spray can be applied to the back of any paper, or clear plastic, to create a custom shield. With any type of adhesive though, care must be taken to be sure none of the adhesive on the material is released from the mask and left behind on the painted surface. It is also important to ensure that the adhesive is not too strong. If the adhesive is very aggressive it will pull up paint when it is removed. Understanding the nature of the adhesive and its intended use, and performing small tests with it beforehand, can save you hours of headaches down the road.

The final photo sequence in this chapter shows how to develop a simple cube shape using frisket as an adhesive mask. Because this material is completely transparent, your drawing can be done either directly on the surface or on the frisket. Here a simple cube shape is laid out. Carefully cut the lines with a sharp, new blade in your X-acto knife. With a brand new blade, the material cuts very cleanly with little pressure.

Once all the lines have been cut, the first panel to the left is removed and a very light fade from the upper right to the lower left is done with black. Unlike the handheld stencils, the entire area is protected by the masking so the airbrush can be held farther away from the surface to produce a very fine, even fade. Next, the right hand panel is removed and the same soft fade from the upper right to the lower left is applied. In this instance it

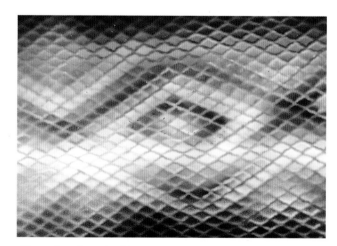

Completed snakeskin pattern.

is all right that the left hand panel is still exposed from the first step. The first panel is the darkest side of the cube so getting it slightly darker with the overspray from the second step will actually make it look more convincing. The third and final step is to remove the top panel and spray it lightly from the top down. Again, the minimal overspray from this step getting on the first two panels will make things look real.

These steps, well thought out and frequently practiced, will enable you to create many other realistic shapes with your airbrush.

Second panel sprayed in.

Cube drawn on paper.

Last panel sprayed in.

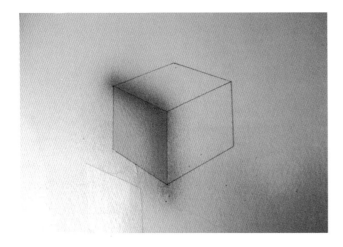

First panel sprayed in.

Completed cube.

Chapter Eighteen

Putting It All Together

Creating A Work of Art

Knowing how an airbrush works will save you much time and aggravation. Keeping the airbrush operating correctly by using good painting habits, you can ensure that your airbrush will be ready to go whenever you are. This chapter will take all those good painting habits and put them together to create a beach scene on a T-shirt.

The supplies you need are as follows:

AIRBRUSH

Traditionally, a T-shirt airbrush is siphon-feed brush with a .5.7mm or medium tip. We, howev-

White highlights added to the water complete the image.

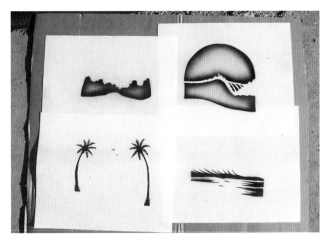

All four of the uncut stencils

Cutting the template with a knife

er, are using a smaller .3mm gravity-feed airbrush for this how-to. This will not only demonstrate the versatility of the airbrush, but it will also show how understanding the airbrush and practicing good techniques can help you do just about anything.

PAINT

For this how-to we are using Createx Colors. This paint is a non-toxic, non-flammable acrylic-based paint specially formulated to bond to fabric permanently once it is heat set.

T-SHIRT

We will be painting on a 100 percent cotton shirt.

STENCIL-EZE STENCIL MATERIAL

We can cut reusable stencils from this felt like material. It is primarily used in embroidery or screen printing, but it makes an excellent airbrushing stencil material as well.

X-ACTO KNIFE

An extra sharp #11 blade will cut through the stencil material quickly and cleanly.

STENCIL BURNER

Some of the shapes that need to be cut out are easier to do with a stencil burner.

T-SHIRT BOARD

A simple 14x16 inch piece of corrugated cardboard will support the shirt during painting.

IRON

A standard household iron can be used after the T-shirt is painted to heat set the colors.

Cutting the template with a stencil burner

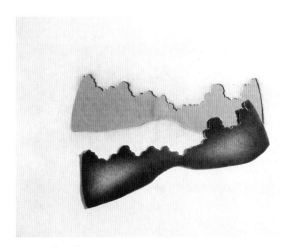

Completed cutout

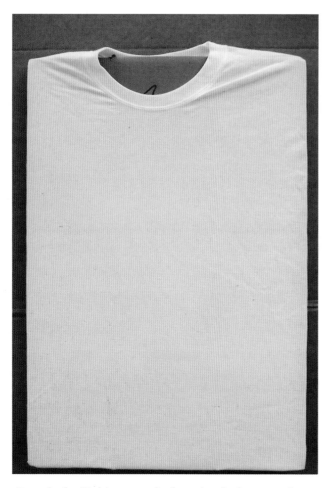

Stretch the T-shirt over the board only far enough to make it lie flat without wrinkles. Do not distort the shape of the shirt.

The beach image we will be painting on this shirt has been divided into four separate elements. This design has come pre-printed as one of the T-Shirt Master Designs from BearAir (see "Sources").

As you progress through this tutorial you will see how any complex image can be broken down into simple pieces.

Each of the four elements used in our demonstration has been printed on a sheet of Stencil-Eze. You can use one of these, or break down an image of your own into its simple elements.

Our first step is to cut the images from all the stencils. A sharp blade does an excellent job cutting smoothly curved shapes. Clean cuts with a blade require the mastery of two techniques.

First, think of the knife blade as a ship's rudder in the water. The sharp edge should always be turned in the direction that the cut is going. This keeps the blade from getting bound up and skipping during the cut.

The second important cutting technique to remember is used in the corners. Simply cutting up to the corner may leave a small piece that won't release the scrap. The solution is to cut slightly beyond the corners so that the cuts overlap. This is extremely important on this design because otherwise the sawtooth shapes of the palm tree leaves would get hung up at all the points.

For cutting such rounded shapes as the clouds, a stencil burner can make this job very easy. Instead of constantly turning the knife blade to follow all the curves, the heated stencil burner can cut everything out by merely tracing around the design.

You can discard all the cutouts except for the clouds. Save that one as we will be using it later.

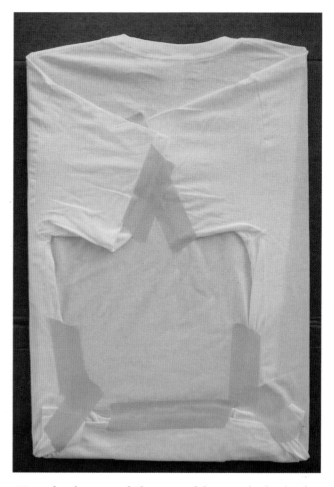

Tape the sleeves and the excess fabric to the back of the board.

When the templates are all cut out, the T-shirt may be stretched over cardboard or foamboard. The board should be just large enough to stretch the shirt smooth, yet not so tight that it distorts the fabric. From there, the arms and extra material can be taped to the back, out of the way.

PAINTING TECHNIQUES USED WHEN WORKING WITH TEMPLATES.

One way to use these T-shirt templates is to spray the backside of each one with a repositionable aerosol adhesive. This will hold the templates in place and keep them from being lifted by the air from the brush. Without the adhesive holding the stencil down, paint can be sprayed underneath, and the edge that results is fuzzy.

You can prevent this underspray without the use of adhesives by using the air from the airbrush to your advantage. When it is positioned so that it sprays with the template (see photos), the air actually helps hold the template in place, leaving a very hard, sharp edge on the painted area. This technique can take a little thought and practice. Constant awareness of the posi-

Spraying against the edge of the template allows the air to push the template up and the paint to underspray.

Spraying with the template holds it down

129

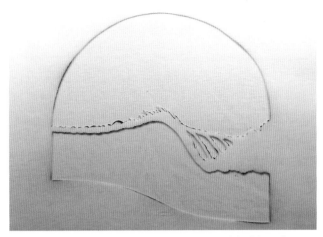

Center the template on the T-shirt and hold it down with stencil tac or your hand.

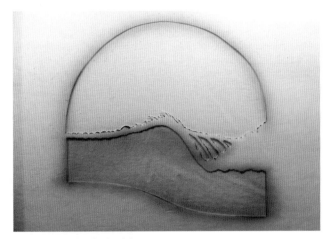

Spraying the light blue.

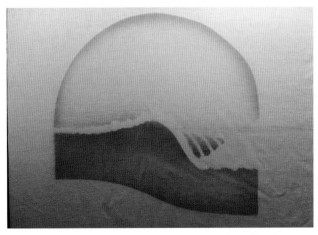

Completed blue section. NOTE: Template has been removed for illustration only; leave in place until you are finished.

tion of the airbrush in relation to the template will dramatically speed up the process of working with hand held templates. Understanding the way an airbrush operates frees you from dependence on set techniques and gives you more creativity and flexibility.

FIRST TEMPLATE

Locate the first template on the shirt about an inch below the collar, and hold it in place with a piece of two inch masking tape. To keep the remainder of the shirt clean during the painting process, you can cover it with a piece of paper taped to the bottom of the template.

Using a primary blue color, a very light fade is applied to the top edge of the template. On this pass the airbrush is kept about 6-8 inches away from the surface of the shirt. The light fade stroke used here ensures that the whole edge is blended together seamlessly.

Another light layer of the same blue is also applied to the lower section. Again using light fade strokes at about 6-8 inches, working with the edge of the template will create a seamless wash. Using controlled fade strokes here will also minimize the dried paint that collects on the needle.

(NOTE: The template in these pictures is frequently removed to show how each finished color step looks. During the actual process however, this template should be left in place until it is no longer needed.)

The next color to be applied through this template is fluorescent pink. While the technique is the same as with the blue, the distance the airbrush is held from the surface is increased to 8-10 inches. The only concern here is to make sure that the painting is done with the edge of the template.

More paint will be applied in this pass because of the distance from the surface, thus increasing the chance of the template being lifted and undersprayed. But, by being farther away, the spray produced is very fine and controlled.

The color to follow the pink is fluorescent yellow. Again, the same techniques that served to apply the blue can be used.

Constant removal of tip dry is essential here to keep things running. Excessive tip dry on an airbrush when working close and with details can cause uneven and diverted spray. Tip dry causes the paint to spit out of the airbrush, and at this distance the droplets can be quite large.

In the next step the wave template is used directly over the first template. The first template continues to mask off the overall shape of the wave while the second template will define the darker areas below the crest.

Normally you could spray blue across the entire open area of the second template and its shape would make the general wave form. However, by using some of the foundational airbrush strokes that we have learned, you can make the entire area look hand painted and not stenciled.

You will fill this area with simple dagger strokes. If you are still working at mastering that one, a line stroke will work equally well here. Take time and work in many of these horizontal blue lines across the entire lower area of this template. You can use a curved line in the wave area above where the curl rises from the water, to give the feel of the wave curling over. Again, use whatever stroke is within your ability here and the template will make up for any imperfections. The template will compensate.

The next step takes a bit of control over the line and dagger strokes but the result can be stunning. The goal here is to blur the hard edges that were created by the previous template. The most successful paintings are those where it is difficult for the viewer to tell what technique was used.

Here, a simple dagger stroke is used, starting within the darker blue area and extending outward. Paint as many as you can until the hard edge left by the last template is gone. When finished, it will appear as if you sprayed in the entire area with freehand dagger strokes. Finally, a light fade of darker blue is applied to the top of the wave inside the curl.

By working in light, controlled layers you can dramatically reduce tip dry and not overdo the application of color. It is much easier to add a bit of color to darken something than to try to fix an area that has received too much paint.

The blue and pink sections are blended together using fade strokes

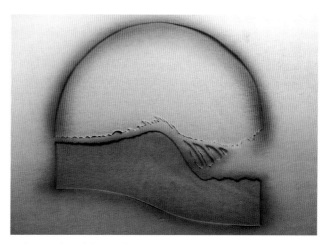

The pink is blended in over the blue

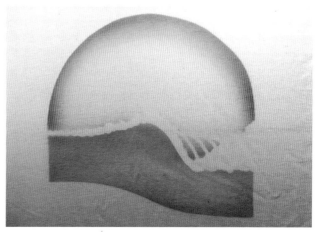

Finished application of the pink shows the wider strokes that result from spraying from a greater distance than the blue. Again, don't remove the template yet.

131

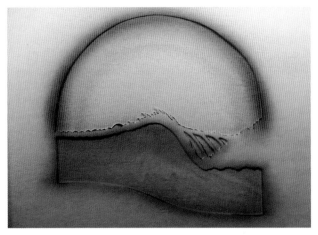

Fluorescent yellow is applied along the outer edge.

Curved dagger strokes that make up the waves.

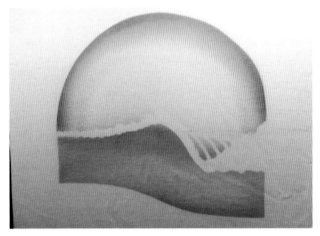

Completed application of the yellow, again show without the template that should remain in place through all the steps so .

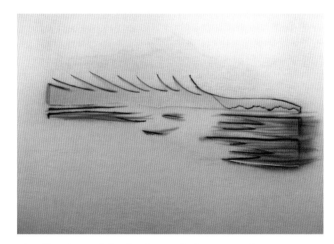

Application of the horizontal dagger strokes.

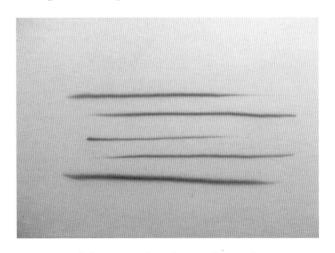

Horizontal dagger strokes that make up the wave texture.

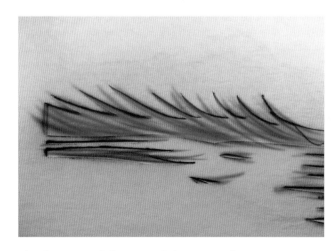

Application of the curved dagger strokes.

132

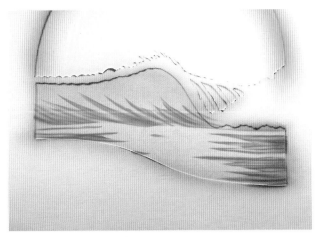

Completed, stenciled wave texture.

Cloud template put in place and cloud texture applied using template cut out.

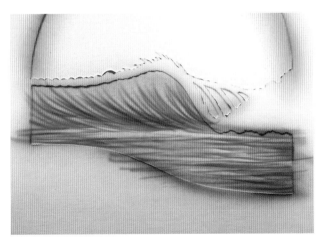

With wave templates removed, extend the dagger strokes in the waves to blend away the edges.

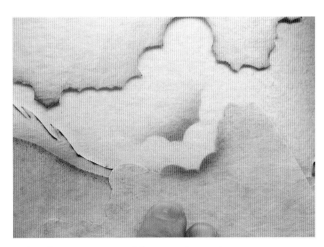

Cloud texture created by template edge.

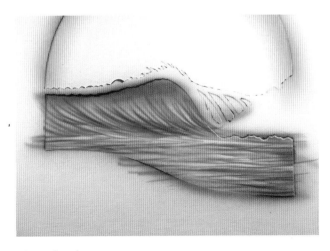

Completed waves.

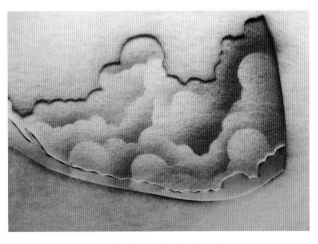

Cloud texture applied to whole cloud area.

Light mist of magenta applied across the whole cloud area to tie it all together.

Completed clouds.

Palm tree template put in position.

From here, place the cloud template over the first template. For the clouds, use a fluorescent magenta. In order to get a cloud texture, use the edges of the cloud cut out from this template. Using a light fade stroke, choose a small section of the edge of the cut out and spray lightly. Move the cut out slightly and spray another section, making sure that things remain varied and none of the shapes overlap. An overlap will make it go from looking like a puffy cloud to a more transparent web.

After the whole section is textured with the cloud shapes, you can lightly go over the entire area with the same magenta to tie it all together. Stay 8-10 inches away and apply the color very lightly until you reach the shade that looks best.

Now you finally can remove all the templates and get a look at the progress you've made on the whole image.

The next step is to position the tree template. The trees act as a border and frame the beach scene. Black is used for the trees and the birds. Even when applying the black in light, controlled layers, the heavy pigment in the paint quickly collects on the needle. Be proactive here and constantly clean away this buildup before it interferes with the operation of the airbrush.

Once the black is put in lightly, the stencil can be removed. Like the dark blue in the waves, the edge of the palm leaves look cut and pasted and some dagger strokes would help them look a bit more natural. As with the dagger strokes in the waves, these are tight and controlled and take a bit of practice to accomplish.

It is a good idea to work these small strokes out on a scrap piece until you feel comfortable. These dagger strokes are small. You start them with the airbrush about 11/2- 2 inches from the surface and end them by practically touching the surface of the shirt. Note the photo that shows these strokes as they radiate from the center of each palm leaf and also from the base of the trunk, giving the impression of grass. Long, light fade strokes along the bottom edge of the image are also put in to suggest the profile of a sand dune on the beach.

The final step to add life to this image is to add some white highlights in the water. Here simple, small highlights are put in the waves by using the dot stroke. Placing them randomly in the center of the water gives the impression of the sun reflecting off the water, and finishes off this beach scene.

This entire project was done using nothing but basic strokes and some simple stencils. Bringing them together resulted in a complete, multicolored image. As your freehand airbrushing skills improve certain templates can be eliminated because it will be faster to simply paint in the desired area without the template. The wave is a great example of this.

If you were able to extend the wave shapes to blur the stenciled edge, you have already gained the skills to paint in the entire area without the templates. With each new job you will be faced with this decision—which steps can you do freehand and which will require templates? Most projects will require some combination of areas that are masked off and others that are simply painted in. Use whichever will produce the results you are looking for while making the most efficient use of your time and effort.

Small dagger strokes are used to extend the palm leaves.

Dagger strokes applied to the right hand tree.

Black is applied through the template in light controlled layers.

Be careful to remove all tip dry during painting to avoid clogging problems.

Chapter Nineteen

Troubleshooting Guide

Common Solutions

One thing is certain, no matter what kind of air-brushing you choose to do things will sometimes go wrong. Occasionally the solution will be simple, an overlooked error that can be found and remedied easily, while other times it will be more challenging. Several changes may be needed to get things back up and running. This chapter is designed to give you a brief outline of some of the most common problems and their possible solutions. Use it as a starting point for the notes you will collect as you discover solutions to your own problems.

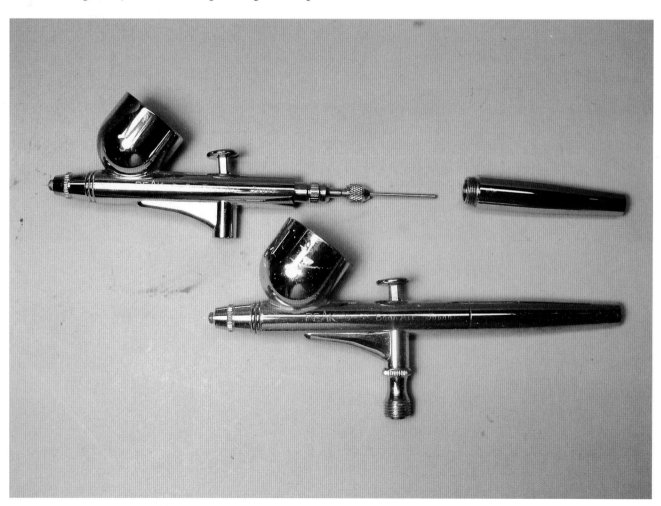

Twin brushes for swapping parts.

Simple things can cause the biggest headaches. Check all connections first.

Check to make sure the compressor is in the "ON" or "AUTO" position.

Keep propellant cans from freezing by placing in warm water.

COMMON PROBLEMS
WITH THE AIR SOURCE

Problem: There is no airflow at airbrush.
Solutions: First make sure the compressor is plugged in and turned on. This sounds so obvious and simple, but most compressors have automatic shut off switches that only allow the motor to run when the pressure drops below a certain level. That means that at least half the time the compressor will seem as if it has turned itself off. A simple check here could save hours of aggravation.

If you are using canned, compressed air, make sure the can has not frozen. As the compressed air is expelled, the can will slowly drop in temperature. This drop in temperature can cause the air valve to freeze up and not function. Simply placing the can in a shallow bowl of warm water will keep things running.

The next thing to check is to be sure the regulator is set to the correct pressure. If you changed airbrushes or hoses the night before you lowered the pressure on the regulator. A simple look will tell you if this is the problem.

Is a hose washer out of place? Some air hoses have small rubber O-rings in their fittings to help create an airtight seal. If one of these O-rings accidentally gets shifted it may actually block the airflow.

Check to see if the regulator is receiving any pressure.

Inspect the hose washer if airbrush is getting no air.

Inspect the hose fittings to see if the Teflon tape is blocking any of the openings.

Air regulator in locked position.

Teflon tape can block airflow. Occasionally, during the application of the Teflon tape to the threads of the airbrush, compressor or air line fittings, the tape can accidentally cover the opening of the hose or fitting it was intended to seal.

Check for a crimped hose. As the airbrush is being constantly picked up and put back down, the hose may become tangled and crimped. Another common crimping issue can happen when your chair leg is set on or rolled over the hose.

Your airbrush may contain incorrect parts. Make certain that you have all the proper, matching parts in your airbrush. Some models have multiple sized, interchangeable tips and needles. A larger nozzle in a smaller air cap will completely shut off the airflow through the brush.

Problem: The regulator will not move, unable to adjust.

Solution: Most regulators have a locking device that keeps the pressure where you set it. If this lock is in place it will not allow the pressure to be adjusted at all. Some regulators have a visible orange ring to let you know that it is unlocked - others do not. Simply pull up on the pressure adjustment of the regulator to make sure it is unlocked.

Problem: The compressor is making funny noises.

Solutions: Noises that compressors make later, but did not make when they were new are an indication of a serious problem that has already happened - or is about to happen to the compressor. If you hear an unfamiliar noise, immediately turn the compressor off. If it is a silent compressor, check to make sure that it has the correct amount of oil.

Any other problems associated with a change in the operating sound are usually issues that should be resolved by the manufacturer. Have all the information—such as the make and model of the compressor, what the conditions were when the problem arose, etc.—on hand when you call. Giving technicians as much info as you can will help them quickly resolve your problem.

Problem: Compressor will not turn on.

Solutions: As before, first make sure that the compressor is plugged in. It sounds silly and obvious, yet plugs can be accidentally knocked loose.

The second thing to look at is the way the compressor was being used before it shut down. Most compressors have thermal switches that are designed to serve as fail-safes, shutting the compressor down if it reaches a dangerous temperature during operation. Simply waiting for the compressor to cool down will reset the switch and allow operation again.

However, if this level of overheating has been reached, you should reconsider whether you have realistic expectations of your compressor. If this safety switch is tripped it is an indicator that you are overworking your compressor. You should consider a stronger model before doing permanent damage.

Problem: Auto-shut-off turns compressor on without the airbrush in operation.

Solution: Air is leaking somewhere in the system. Carefully examining all the places where threaded connections are made will probably turn up a leak. A great way to test the seals in your compressor and air lines is to mix some water and a small amount of dish soap in a bowl. Brush a small bit of the solution on the seal that you are checking. If bubbles appear, you know that you have a leak. Remove the fitting, apply Teflon plumber's tape and reconnect. If however, you find that the air leak is from a non-threaded connection contact the manufacturer to discuss your options.

COMMON AIRBRUSH PROBLEMS

Problem: Trigger won't move or is stuck.

Solutions: Several things can cause the trigger to stop functioning. If it is loose and just flops back and forth, remove the handle and loosen the needle chuck. The trigger should bounce back to its closed position. On most airbrushes, if the needle chuck is over-tightened it will cause the needle to bind up.

If this doesn't solve the problem, remove the needle and clean it thoroughly, as well as the passageway the needle goes through. Dried paint buildup in this passageway is the Number One cause of poor trigger action.

The same solution holds true if the trigger's up and down movement is sluggish. Disassembly and cleaning of the air valve, and the air valve pin, will ensure the system works properly.

Problem: Needle is stuck and cannot be removed.

Solutions: Paint has been allowed to dry in the airbrush and is acting like glue on the needle. Begin by cleaning as much of the dried paint out of the brush as possible. Soak the front end of the airbrush

Air regulator in unlocked position.

Checking an Iwata Micron C for air leaks with soap - this photo shows leaks in the aircap.

Clean out the bowl with a brush. This solvent brush will work with any cleaner.

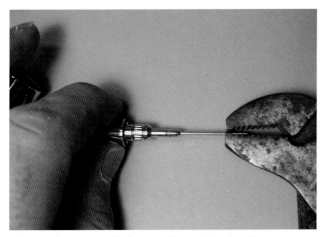

Use a pliers to pull the needle straight back.

Make sure the feed stem in the bottle does not touch the bottom.

Check to see if the breather hole in the cap is blocked with dried paint.

to loosen things up. Once the cleaning is done, try to remove the needle again. If it is still stuck, grab the end of the needle firmly with a pair of pliers and pull straight back with steady, even pressure until the needle is free. Continue the complete breakdown and cleaning.

Problem: Paint is not coming out of the airbrush.

Solutions: First check to see if you have run out of paint in the bottle or cup. Don't laugh, it has happened to us all! Second, with a siphon-feed airbrush, inspect the feed tube in the bottle to make sure it is not hitting the bottom of the bottle, or has an obstruction in it. Also check the breather hole in the top of the bottle. If paint dries in that hole and blocks it then a vacuum is formed in the bottle and paint will not be allowed to flow.

In a side-feed or gravity-feed airbrush look for dried paint chunks that block the feed. Next look at the paint itself. Make sure it is not too thick for the type of airbrush you are using, and make sure that the pressure is high enough for paint as well.

Problem: Paint flow is too fast and flooding.

Solution: Make sure the paint is not too thin and the pressure is not too high. Again, review what you are expecting the airbrush to do for you. If you are trying to get super-fine detail with a .7mm siphon-feed brush, then you will encounter this flooding problem often.

Problem: Spider webbing occurs.

Solutions: Spider webbing is what you get when paint floods onto the surface very quickly and is pushed around by the air before it has a chance to dry. Several things can cause it to happen more frequently - working with a light viscosity material at high pressure, working on a non-porous surface or working with a large high flow nozzle.

Spider webbing can be prevented by changing any of the variables listed above, although the real fix to this problem will come with increased airbrush control. The application of paint in light, controlled layers will eliminate spider webbing almost immediately by simply allowing the paint to dry as it hits the surface.

Problem: Paint has a grainy spray pattern.

Solutions: Several things can cause a grainy spray pattern. The first thing to do is be sure the viscosity of the paint matches the size of the airbrush. If the paint is very thick, the smaller airbrushes will be unable to atomize it properly and the spray pattern will be grainy. Very low air pressure also will cause this grainy spray pattern.

One final thing that can cause this type of spray pattern is an obstruction in the paint flow. This can be anything from a chunk of dried paint blocking the feed circuit, or even the points of a needle crown cap in some instances. Basically, anything that is introduced into the atomized paint flow can cause that atomized paint to recollect as larger paint droplets.

Problem: Paint sprays with an irregular skipping pattern.

Solutions: Irregular or skipping spray patterns can be caused by excess buildup of dried paint, both inside the nozzle and on the opening of the nozzle cap. A thorough cleaning of those parts will nearly always cure this problem. However, a split nozzle or bent needle can also cause an irregular spray pattern. Careful inspection of these parts and repair or replacement will also remedy this problem.

Problem: Paint sprays with a regular skipping pattern.

Solutions: While an irregular skipping pattern can usually be traced back to a paint problem, a regular or even skipping pattern is usually an indication of a mechanical problem. Nearly every time this happens it is due to the vacuum seal being broken on the air cap. Air is getting into the cap and interfering with the airbrush's ability to draw paint from the cup or bottle. The solution is to first visually inspect the threads on both the air cap and the body of the airbrush itself. A damaged air cap should be replaced.

Damaged threads in the body of the airbrush are usually not repairable. If the threads are fine, then a sealant such as beeswax can be used to restore the seal.

Having multiple airbrushes of the same model can be both a time saver and an invaluable repair tool. Having two identical airbrushes gives you the ability to swap out parts, one by one, from the good brush to the bad brush until you find the exact part that is causing the issue.

Problems pop up all the time. Some of them are subtle and require both thought and experimentation to resolve. Keep in mind the fundamental ways in which the airbrush works and you will be able to systematically eliminate possible causes until you find the right solution.

Spider webs

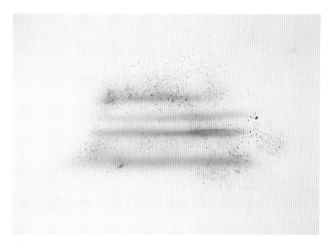
Grainy/spitting pattern.

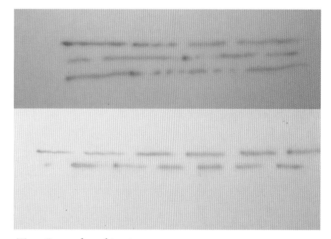
Top: Irregular skipping
Bottom: Regular skipping

AIR BRUSHING 101

Airbrushing 101 presents a series of start-to-finish projects, each painted by a different artist, and each designed to illustrate a different type of airbrushing. Author Doug Mitchel and the artists in the book introduce a wide range of airbrushing categories, including: fire art/illustration, T-shirts, automotive, fingernails, body and face painting, hip hop and model painting.

All the start-to-finish photo sequences are designed for first-time airbrush users. In addition to the sequences, this book illustrates the basic strokes that form the foundation for nearly all airbrush art. Doug Mitchel uses interviews to explore the way in which each artist learned his or her skills, what type of paint they prefer, how they adjust their airbrush, and how to avoid the typical beginner's mistakes.

Ten Chapters   144 Pages $27.95   Over 400 photos, 100% color

ADVANCED AIRBRUSH ART

Like a video done with still photography, this new book is made up entirely of photo sequences that illustrate each small step in the creation of an airbrushed masterpiece. Watch as well-known masters like Vince Goodeve, Chris Cruz, Steve Wizard and Nick Pastura start with a sketch and end with a NASCAR helmet or motorcycle tank covered with graphics, murals, pinups or all of the above.

Interviews explain each artist's preference for paint and equipment, and secrets learned over decades of painting. Projects include a chrome eagle surrounded by reality flames, a series of murals, and a variety of graphic designs.
This is a great book for anyone who takes their airbrushing seriously and wants to learn more.

Ten Chapters   144 Pages $27.95   Over 400 photos, 100% color

PRO AIRBRUSH TIPS & TECHNIQUES WITH VINCE GOODEVE

Written by well-known Airbrush artist Vince Goodeve, this book explains a lifetime's worth of learning. Follow Vince through multiple photo sequences that explain his choice of color, sense of design and preference for tools and materials. Chapters explain shop set up and preparations of the metal canvas. Ten start-to-finish sequences walk the reader through Vince's airbrush work

with both motorcycles and cars. Projects include simple graphics as well as complex and intricate designs.
Accustomed to teaching, Vince uses a style that is easy to follow and understand. His enthusiasm for the airbrush comes through, making the text easy to follow. Vince has something to say to all airbrush artists – whether beginner or advanced.

Fifteen Chapters   144 Pages $27.95   Over 500 photos, 100% color

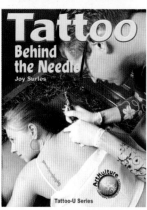

TATTOOS THROUGH TIME

Tattoos Through Time takes the reader from the early days of sailor tattoos to current, colorful and elaborate, tattoos. Told by the seasoned artists who pushed the envelope to the current state of the art, this book uses old photos and interviews with the early artists to explain the evolution of the art. Who was the first to use color, how have the inks changed, what are the inks and pigments made from, how light-fast are the materials? This new

book explains all these questions. Photos of early tattoo parlors show in graphic detail how much better the hygiene is today.
For anyone with an interest in Tattoos, this book gives an accurate look at "the good old days" and how we've gone from those not-so-great practices to the beautiful and safe art we enjoy today.
Available, spring of 2009.

Ten Chapters   144 Pages $27.95   Over 500 photos, 100% color

Wolfgang Publication Titles

For a current list visit our website at www.wolfpub.com

PAINT EXPERT

How Airbrushes Work	$27.95
Air Brushing 101	$27.95
Adv. Custom Motorcycle Painting	$27.95
Advanced Airbrush Art	$27.95
Advanced Custom Painting Techniques	$27.95
Advanced Custom Painting Techniques (Spanish)	$27.95
Advanced Pinstripe Art	$27.95
Kustom Painting Secrets	$19.95
Custom Paint & Graphics	$27.95
Pro Airbrush Techniques	$27.95
How to Paint Barns & Buildings	$27.95

BIKER BASICS

Sheet Metal Fabrication	$27.95
How to FIX American V-Twin MC	$27.95

HOP-UP EXPERT

How to Hop & Customize your Bagger	$27.95
How to Hop & Customize your Softail	$27.95
How toCustomize Your Star	$27.95

CUSTOM BUILDER SERIES

Adv Custom Motorcycle Wiring	$27.95
Adv Custom Motorcycle Assembly & Fabrication	$27.95
Adv. Custom Motorcycle Chassis	$27.95
How to Build a Cheap Chopper	$27.95
How to Build a Chopper	$27.95

SHEET METAL

Advanced Sheet Metal Fabrication	$27.95
Ultimate Sheet Metal Fabrication	$19.95

OLD SKOOL SKILLS

Barris: Grilles,Scoops, Fins and Frenching (Vol. 2)	$24.95
Barris: Flames Scallops, Paneling and Striping (Vol. 4)	$24.95

HOT ROD BASICS

How to Air Condition Your Hot Rod	$27.95
How to Chop Tops	$24.95
How to Wire your Hot Rod	$27.95

MOTORCYCLE RESTORATION SERIES

Triumph Resotoration	$29.95
Triumph MC Restoration Pre-Unit	$29.95

ILLUSTRATED HISTORY

Triumph Motorcycles	$32.95

HOME SHOP

How to Paint Tractors & Trucks	$27.95

TATTOO U Series

Tattoo- From Idea to Ink	$27.95
Tattoos Behind the Needle	$27.95
Advanced Tattoo Art	$27.95
Body Painting	$27.95

COMPOSITE GARAGE

Composite Materials	$27.95

JAN 0 4 2010

Sources

Airbrush.com
www.airbrush.com

Andy Penaluna
www.andypenaluna.com

Armadillo Art—Frisk
P.O. Box A
Belle Mead, NJ 08502
USA
www.armadilloart.com

Badger Airbrush Company
9128 West Belmont Ave.
Franklin Park, IL 60131
USA
847-678-3104
www.badgerairbrush.com

BearAir
20 Hampden Dr.
Unit 2R
South Easton, MA 02375
USA
800-232-7247
www.bearair.com

Createx Colors
14 Airport Park Road
East Granby, CT. 06026
USA
800-243-2712
www.createxcolors.com

DeVilbiss
USA
800-445-3988
www.devilbiss.com

EFBE
Friedrich Boldt GmbH
Sudewiesenstr. 28
D-30880 Laatzen
Germany
+49 (0) 5 11 / 32 34 20
www.efbe-airbrush.de

Frisk Film
330-785-0435
www.getpainted.com

Golden Artist Colors, Inc.
188 Bell Road
New Berlin, NY 13411-9527
USA
800-959-6543
www.goldenpaints.com

Harder & Steenbeck
GmbH & Co. KG
Im Hegen 3
D-22113 Oststeinbek
Germany
+49 (40) 87 87 989 30
www.hansa-airbrush.de

HOLBEIN Works, Ltd.
1-3-20, Kamikosaka
Higashiosaka-city, Osaka 577-0806
Japan
81-6-6723-1555
www.holbein-works.co.jp

House of Kolor
210 Crosby St.
Picayune, MS 39466
USA
601-798-4229
www.houseofkolor.com

Inovart – Precision Aire
2304 58th St. East
Bradenton, FL 34203
USA
941-751-2324
www.inovart.com

Iwata Medea, Inc.
PO Box 17408
Portland, OR 97217
USA
503.253.7308
www.iwata-medea.com

Learn Airbrush and Design
3912 View Point Way
Lafayette, CO 80026
USA
303-828-0370
www.learnairbrush.com

Paasche Airbrush Company
4311 North Normandy Avenue
Chicago, IL 60634-1395
USA
773-867-9191
www.paascheairbrush.com

PPG World Headquarters
One PPG Place
Pittsburgh, Pennsylvania 15272
USA
(412) 434-3131
www.ppg.com

Fuso Seiki Co., Ltd.
Richpen
12-17, Honkomagome 6 Chome,
Bunkyo-ku, Tokyo
113-0021
Japan
+81-3-3947-1334
www.richpen.com

Silentaire Compressors
8614 Veterans Memorial Dr.
Houston, Texas 77088
USA
832 327-7452
www.silentaire.com

Taiwan Airbrushes & Equipments Co., Ltd.
Sogolee
No. 8, Hsiao Yang Mei,
Yung Ning Li,
Yang Mei, Taoyuan
Taiwan
886-3-475-5141
www.sogolee.com

Steven Leahy
www.stevenleahy.com

Tamiya America, Inc.
36 Discovery #200
Irvine, CA 92618
USA
800 TAMIYA-A
www.tamiyausa.com

Testors
440 Blackhawk Park Drive
Rockford, IL 61104
USA
800 962-6654
www.testors.com